CREATING INCLUSIVE ONLINE COMMUNITIES

CREATING INCLUSIVE ONLINE COMMUNITIES

Practices That Support and Engage Diverse Students

Sharla E. Berry

Foreword by Kathryn E. Linder

NEW YORK AND LONDON

First published 2022 by Stylus Publishing, LLC.

First Edition, 2022

Published 2023 by Routledge
605 Third Avenue, New York, NY 10017
4 Park Square, Milton Park, Abingdon, Oxon OX14 4RN

Routledge is an imprint of the Taylor & Francis Group, an informa business

Copyright © 2022 Taylor & Francis Group.

All rights reserved. No part of this book may be reprinted or reproduced or utilised in any form or by any electronic, mechanical, or other means, now known or hereafter invented, including photocopying and recording, or in any information storage or retrieval system, without permission in writing from the publishers.

Notice:
Product or corporate names may be trademarks or registered trademarks, and are used only for identification and explanation without intent to infringe.

Library of Congress Cataloging-in-Publication Data
Names: Berry, Sharla E., author.
Title: Creating inclusive online communities : practices that support and
    engage diverse students / Sharla E. Berry ; foreword by Kathryn E. Linder.
Description: First edition. | Sterling, Virginia : Stylus Publishing, LLC,
    2022. | Includes bibliographical references and index.
Identifiers: LCCN 2022038536 |
    ISBN 9781642673050 (paperback) | ISBN 9781642673043 (cloth)
Subjects: LCSH: Education, Higher--Effect of technological innovations
    on--United States. | Web-based instruction--Social aspects--United
    States. | Minorities--Education (Higher)--United States. | Nontraditional
    college students--United States.
Classification: LCC LB2395.7 .B466 2022 |
    DDC 371.33/44678--dc23/eng/20220922
LC record available at https://lccn.loc.gov/2022038536

ISBN 13: 978-1-64267-304-3 (hbk)
ISBN 13: 978-1-64267-305-0 (pbk)
ISBN 13: 978-1-00-344378-0 (ebk)

DOI: 10.4324/9781003443780

CONTENTS

	FOREWORD *Kathryn E. Linder*	vii
	PREFACE	ix
	ACKNOWLEDGMENTS	xiii
1	DEFINING COMMUNITY The Foundation of an Inclusive and Engaging Course or Program	1
2	WHAT MAKES A STRONG ONLINE INSTRUCTOR? Creating Inclusive Communities	21
3	THE ROLE OF TECHNOLOGY IN THE ONLINE CLASSROOM	38
4	ASYNCHRONOUS TEACHING PRACTICES THAT SUPPORT ONLINE COMMUNITY	63
5	SYNCHRONOUS TEACHING PRACTICES THAT SUPPORT ONLINE COMMUNITY	84
	CONCLUSION	99
	APPENDIX A: CULTIVATING COMMUNITY DURING A PANDEMIC Online Teaching, Emergency Remote Instruction, and Pandemic Pedagogy	103
	REFERENCES	109
	ABOUT THE AUTHOR	119
	INDEX	121

FOREWORD

Recently, I had the opportunity to lead a series of conversations on my campus around the future of digital education at our institution. These conversations included a range of community members such as faculty, staff, administrative and academic leaders, and—of course—our students.

One conversation that I had with a group of students really stuck out to me. They talked about their challenges with feeling a sense of community in their online and remote courses. Some of this had to do with communication challenges. For example, they talked about sending emails "into the void" and struggling to talk with faculty outside of face-to-face environments. They also described how intimidated they were to approach their faculty, especially those students who were transferring into our institution later in their academic journey or who identified as first-generation college learners.

Even with all the technologies that we have, and the experiences that we have gained with using new tools during the recent pandemic period, many students and faculty still struggle with building community in online courses and programs. Moreover, many of the learners at our institution are what some people have called the "new majority learner," or the population of students that higher education was not originally meant to serve. These historically marginalized and underrepresented students may struggle even more to find community at our campuses and institutions.

To be sure, building community inside and outside of the online classroom presents challenges for our students and our faculty. When I talk with faculty about this challenge, what do they ask for the most? Examples! They want to see what the best practices look like. They want models for changes that they can make in their own classrooms.

When Sharla Berry shared this book idea with me, I knew it would be filling an important gap in our literature. We need more tactics to share with our instructors for how they can cocreate community with their students in both synchronous and asynchronous online environments. Moreover, we need these tactics to be accessible, creative, and varied.

This book answers that charge.

Enhancing our classrooms with technology will never take away the personal and human element of learning. Building community with learners is one of the most important jobs that our faculty have. Strong communities help learners to know their role in the classroom and at our institutions. They also help students to have a place to ask their questions when they get stuck, to feel a sense of belongingness, and to develop important relationships with mentors and peers.

Even more important, this is one of the key guides in the field that considers the role that race, sex, gender, class, and ability play in our online learning communities. Having these more expanded conversations around diversity, equity, and inclusion will only become more important in the years to come as higher education continues to become more diverse.

The practical and actionable strategies in this book offer readers a range of possibilities for changes they can make in their online classrooms and programs immediately. Whether you are an instructor, a staff member who supports students, a staff member who supports faculty in their teaching, or an administrator providing campus-wide leadership, you will find something here to improve equitable and inclusive community-building at your institution.

—Kathryn E. Linder
Associate Vice Chancellor for Digital Strategies and Learning
University of Colorado Denver
April 2022

PREFACE

In 2020, the COVID-19 pandemic forced many American education institutions to provide some form of distance education. Physical distancing mandates created restrictions on face-to-face learning, as large gatherings were discouraged in an attempt to slow the spread of the virus. Faced with an emerging and evolving threat, institutions have been forced to rapidly prepare for distance learning (Hodges et al., 2020). It is too soon to determine the lasting effect of the rapid shift to online learning on the higher education landscape.

While the move toward online learning will be temporary at some institutions, others will use this experience to permanently expand their footprint in the online learning space. Other institutions may take a middle road, offering more online courses rather than switching to fully online programs. Some institutions will find that online learning provides them with opportunities to expand offerings to different students, and to possibly generate more revenue. Either way, online learning is likely to be a major part of the higher education landscape for the foreseeable future.

It is important to note that online learning was already a significant part of higher education prior to the pandemic. According to NCES, in fall 2018, there were over 19 million students enrolled in degree-granting courses at postsecondary institutions, and nearly 7 million in distance education courses. A total of 16.6% of American students in degree-granting postsecondary institutions were in exclusively distance education programs. Whether institutions have been players in the online space for some time or whether they are just entering the space, it will be important for faculty, administrators, and staff to continue thinking about how to develop inclusive and engaging online courses and programs.

Organization of the Book

In this book, readers will explore the ways in which postsecondary stakeholders can strengthen online teaching and learning. Using community as a framing concept, readers will learn strategies for teaching in synchronous, asynchronous, and blended environments, and considerations for using various aspects of a learning management system (LMS) and virtual classroom to support learning. Each chapter includes considerations for supporting students from historically recognized and marginalized backgrounds. Additionally, each chapter includes recommendations for administrators and support staff; including instructional designers, faculty developers, and staff in centers for teaching and learning. Readers will find that this volume provides them with ideas and strategies that are practical and actionable, and support them in creating inclusive and engaging learning communities that serve diverse students.

This book can be read in chapter order, or readers can skip around, focusing on chapters and sections that are relevant to them in the present moment. Chapter 1 reviews the core components of community, as well as the elements that support and undermine it. Chapter 2 outlines what makes a strong online instructor. Chapter 3 explores the ways in which technology supports community in both blended and fully online programs, as well as the impact of synchronous, asynchronous, and hybrid learning on students' sense of community. Strategies for teaching in asynchronous and synchronous courses are outlined in chapters 4 and 5.

Audience

Instructors who teach hybrid or fully online courses are the primary audience for this book. However, this book also holds important pieces of information for administrators, instructional designers, and instructional support staff who work in collaboration with online instructors. Staff who read this book will find suggestions for how to communicate with faculty around the various technological and pedagogical elements that support a robust online course. Practitioners in centers for teaching and learning, faculty development, and information technology will find that this material provides a bridge between the work that they do and the work that faculty do. These stakeholders, who likely have a deep understanding of teaching and learning, will find ways to communicate their expertise to faculty who may be newer to the online teaching experience.

Academic leaders will also find this book to be a useful guide. Leaders, including department chairs, deans, and those in senior academic leadership will uncover considerations for teaching excellence both at the classroom and program level. As such, this volume is a vital tool for administrators that are looking for faculty development resources that consider the diverse, multifaceted, and evolving nature of online courses and programs.

Additionally, faculty, staff, and leadership who are committed to learning about how diversity, equity, and inclusion influence online students' sense of community will find this book to be an asset. This volume highlights the unique needs of Black, Indigenous, and People of Color (BIPOC) students, and also acknowledges the experiences of women, LGBTQ students, low-income students, and students with disabilities. Readers will find clear steps for improving academic experiences and outcomes for these students and for all students.

This book is also beneficial for researchers and scholar-practitioners who are interested in studying and improving online teaching and learning. The nuanced perspective on the differences between synchronous, asynchronous, and hybrid instruction will be highly relevant for thinkers who are looking for greater analysis on the role of modality in the educational experience. Additionally, researchers and scholar-practitioners who are looking for frameworks of online community that consider diversity, equity, and inclusion will find that this book provides an intersectional lens by which to explore the online learning experiences of students from different racial and ethnic backgrounds, varying socioeconomic positions, a wide range of gendered experiences, and the experiences of students with disabilities. This broad and inclusive perspective will be vital for both researchers and practitioners who are committed to improving students' experiences in online courses and programs.

ACKNOWLEDGMENTS

Writing a book undoubtedly requires support, encouragement, and assistance from many people. I would like to thank my editor, Sarah Burrows, for her guidance and assistance throughout this process. I'd also like to thank Katie Linder for her support and counsel, and for making the connections that made this book possible. Thank you to Arthur E. Hernández for your encouragement, especially during the early stages of the book. Thank you to Loredana Carson for thoughtfully reviewing my work. On a more personal note, I would like to thank my family for their support, including my mother, Vicki Phillips, my father, the late Bertelle Berry, and my grandmother, the late Elois Phillips. I dedicate this work to the memory of my brother, Omari Miles, and to his children, Baylee, Reign, and KaliDream. May they, and all who encounter this work, be held in supportive, sustaining communities.

I

DEFINING COMMUNITY

The Foundation of an Inclusive and Engaging Course or Program

Community is a vast and complex concept. Community can be understood in terms of its boundaries (where it begins and where it ends) or its membership characteristics, as well as the experiences individuals have when they are in a shared space. In this book, *community* is defined as an activity center where students have feelings of membership and receive social, emotional, academic, or professional support (Ke & Hoadley, 2009; Lai, 2015; Yuan & Kim, 2014). This definition is important because it allows practitioners to consider what students *feel* when they are in community as well as what they *do* collaboratively.

Feelings of community can take many forms. McMillan and Chavis (1986) focus on four feelings that are central to community—membership, influence, fulfillment of needs, and shared emotional connection. *Membership* refers to the feeling that one belongs to a group. *Influence* is the feeling that one's membership matters to the group members, and that one can effect change in the group. *Fulfillment of needs* refers to the feeling that the group provides support for its members' individual and shared goals. A *shared emotional connection* is a feeling that one has relationships with group members where positive feelings are reciprocated.

Researchers and practitioners have focused on other feelings that are central to community as well. For example, *belonging* has been noted as a key component of community. Strayhorn (2012), drawing on Rosenberg & McCullogh (1981) wrote that a *sense of belonging* "refers to a feeling of connectedness, that one is important or matters to others." He further writes that "the absence of a sense of belonging is typically described as a sense of alienation, rejection, social isolation, loneliness, or 'marginality,' all feelings that have been associated with adverse mental health outcomes" (Strayhorn, 2012, p. 2).

These feelings that encompass community do not develop organically, especially when students are separated by physical distance. Instead, feelings of community are cultivated through the intentional efforts of students, faculty, and staff to work collaboratively, show up authentically, and participate fully in teaching and learning.

The aforementioned definition of community also allows us to focus on the type of work that occurs in communities. This book focuses on educational communities, the kind that occur in formal academic courses and degree-granting academic programs. The formal structure and function of educational communities is what differentiates online educational communities from other types of communities, such as interest communities, professional communities, or communities of practice (Carlen & Jobring, 2005). The work of these communities is, on its face, clear. Students are pursuing a shared goal, which is course and/or degree completion. However, simply being in the same cohort, course, or program together does not constitute being in a learning community. Students must have shared goals and work together to complete educational artifacts that reflect their shared goals (Lai, 2015). In a community, the collaborative activities resonate in ways that are both personal and professional. Students in communities do not just connect over academic work, they connect in ways that enrich their lives (Berry, 2017b).

The experience of community is fluid, flexible, and subjective, and depends as much on structure and formality as on students' personal evaluation of their experience. While community can sound like a fluffy concept, there are many steps that faculty, staff, and administrators can take to make it more concrete. This book explores the teaching strategies that create community, as well as the academic and extracurricular experiences (activities, course structure, pedagogical strategies) that contribute to feelings of connection and closeness in online courses and programs.

The work of creating community belongs to everyone connected to an academic program. Instructors can lay the foundation for community by creating norms around experiences that support authenticity and collaboration. Administrators can support learning communities by preparing instructors to engage all students, and by providing extracurricular support for online students. Instructional designers can help faculty leverage technology to develop dynamic learning experiences that maximize student participation. Faculty developers can provide training and guidance on best practices for online teaching and learning. Other staff can support students' sense of community by making sure that all students feel connected, supported, and engaged in the online program. Everyone has a role to play in creating and maintaining community. This book offers strategies and perspectives for how a range of stakeholders might more thoroughly engage in the work of creating and supporting community in online courses and programs.

Why Does Community Matter? The Academic and Social Benefits of Community

Research has found that a sense of community has social, emotional and academic benefits for students, regardless of the program structure or setting. In *Classrooms as Communities*, Tinto (1997) wrote that the more connected students feel to instructors and peers, "the greater their acquisition of knowledge and development of skills" (p. 600). Tinto argued that strong interpersonal connections, positive interactions with instructors, and collaborative engagement with peers all contributed to feelings of belongingness and support within the academic environment, which in turn supported learning. In a nationally representative study, Gopalan and Brady (2020) found that a sense of belonging was a predictor of increased persistence and engagement, as well as better mental health for 4-year students.

Community is both an indication of and a contributing factor to student engagement (Brown & Bursdal, 2012; Torres-Harding et al., 2015). Students who are more engaged in the institution are more likely to feel a sense of community, and students with a strong sense of community are more likely to participate in and engage with their institution (Price & Tovar, 2014). There are many ways to consider what engagement means. Engagement can be intellectual, referring to deep and authentic interactions with curriculum and instructors. Engagement can also be activity-based, and refer to student participation in learning opportunities, extracurricular offerings, and support services. Engagement also refers to the deep connections students make with peers, including their participation in formal programming offered by the institution, involvement in affinity-based networks, and simply through having friendships with peers at their institution. It is hard to think of an aspect of participation, academic or social, that does not require engagement and is not bolstered by a sense of community.

Rovai (2003) found that online students also experienced deeper academic engagement when they felt a sense of community, and that they were more likely to persist in an academic program than their more socially isolated peers. Berry (2017b) found that online students who felt they were in a community were more likely to give and receive academic, social, and emotional support to peers, including career and family advice, tutoring, and other academic support.

A sense of community has social and emotional benefits as well. In a survey of nearly 700 students, Stubb et al. (2011) found that a sense of community can act as a buffer against feelings of stress, anxiety, isolation, and burnout. Pyhältö et al. (2009) found that feelings of membership in a community can be a source of empowerment for emotionally overwhelmed students, and can help them manage stress and exhaustion. Stubb et al. (2011) and Pyhältö et al. (2009) found that students who felt they were in a community received psychological benefits from their membership, including encouragement, inspiration, academic assistance, and emotional support.

Characteristics of a Learning Community

The core features of a learning community include:

- membership, influence, fulfillment of needs, shared emotional connection (McMillan & Chavis, 1986)
- a sense of belonging and connectedness (Rosenberg & McCullough, 1981)
- shared collaboration around learning goals (Berry, 2017b)
- student engagement (Berry, 2017b)
- equity and inclusion (Bensimon and Malcolm, 2012)

Challenges to Community

Communities are not value-neutral. Communities can be both inclusive to some and exclusive of others. Underrepresented students and those from historically marginalized backgrounds can experience marginalization and exclusion from online courses and programs. Sometimes, these experiences take the form of microaggressions, such as being ignored in discussion threads or over-talked in oral discussions. Other times, these experiences can be more overt, and can include discrimination and harassment. Scholars have used the term *the outsider within* to describe the peripheral role that minoritized and marginalized students play in learning communities (Collins, 1986). Underrepresented students may form their own communities to navigate their experiences as "outsiders." Still, the marginalization that minoritized students can experience in academic spaces can have adverse impacts on learning and overall well-being.

It is important for educators to consider the ways in which the online community in their program can be inclusive and supportive for some students, but exclusionary for others. It is also important for educators to consider that some students may experience both inclusion and exclusion simultaneously, finding support in some aspects of the academic program, and experiencing exclusion in other parts of it. Community is not an either/or experience, it is complex, contextual, and constantly shifting. By taking a more critical look at what community is, how it occurs, and who experiences it; faculty, administrators, and staff put themselves in a position to actually create more inclusive online courses and programs.

External factors can present challenges to community as well. Natural disasters, instances of mass violence, and pandemics can force institutions to rapidly change delivery methods and instructional practices. Appendix A provides considerations for emergency remote instruction and online teaching during a pandemic and other disruptive and challenging events.

Frameworks for Understanding Online Community

Researchers and practitioners have used many frameworks to understand how online communities work. In the section that follows, some common frameworks will be explored and their limitations will be considered.

The Community of Inquiry Framework

Community and its benefits are relatively easy to understand, but harder to cultivate. Many factors contribute to students' sense of community, though some are more widely understood and explored than others. Online practitioners and researchers in the field of online learning have often used the community of inquiry (COI) as a framework to understand the online experience (Garrison et al., 2001). The COI framework suggests that a students' sense of community in an online classroom is informed by the cultivation of three interdependent elements, which they call "presences." These include *teaching presence, social presence,* and *cognitive presence.* Instructors can cultivate teaching presence through the way they structure and facilitate their online courses, social presence through the ways in which they engage students and help facilitate peer interactions, and cognitive presence through reflective learning activities.

The COI provides a useful starting point for understanding how community is formed in online courses. First, it helps practitioners recognize that teaching and learning online are very different experiences than teaching and learning in face-to-face environments. Second, it provides a neat organizing schema for instructors and administrators to consider the significant elements of online learning. The focus on the relationship between instructional and social practices offers clear guideposts for faculty development. Finally, the COI framework highlights the centrality of peer-to-peer interaction in the online student experience. This is important because some students and faculty view online learning as an independent, autodidactic experience. While online learning offers a significant measure of autonomy for learners, the COI framework and the research that has used it suggest that interaction and collaboration play a critical role in student success.

Theory of Persistence in Distance Education Programs

While the COI framework is a helpful starting point for understanding community, it has its limitations. Online learning communities are not created in a vacuum. They are influenced significantly by a range of contextual factors that surround the classroom, including individual and program-level factors. Rovai's (2003) theory of persistence in distance education programs provides some insight into what those factors might be. Rovai argues that like all students, online students' sense of community is influenced by students' precollege experiences, during college experiences, and life events. Precollege experiences include academic preparedness and technology skills. Life events include things like birth, death, divorce, pandemics, or loss of employment, as well as a range of personal experiences that might impact students' persistence or engagement in the academic program. In his articulation of the experiences that impact students' during college, Rovai presents a more expansive portrait of what impacts students' sense of community than many online scholars. While a sense of community, labeled here as a COI, in an online class is a central factor, it is one of several. Other factors that impact students' sense of community include technology that enhances student communication, positive interactions with faculty in and outside of classes, and successful engagement with a range of student support services.

One distinct advantage of Rovai's model is that it looks at student experiences in online *programs,* rather than focusing on students' experiences in online *courses.* Given that 14% of undergraduate students and 30% of graduate students are enrolled exclusively in distance education courses (U.S. Department of Education, 2021), this distinction is helpful in understanding students' experiences. By considering online teaching and learning at the program level, educators and researchers can see how students' experiences both within and across courses impact their sense of community. Additionally, a program-level perspective helps individuals consider the impact of student support services on online students' sense of community.

Berry's Integrated Framework for Community in Online Courses and Programs

Both the COI framework and Rovai's theory of persistence in distance education programs offer great insight into the elements that shape online students' sense of community. More contemporary research has suggested that online students can engage in community-building in ways that can be invisible to researchers (Berry, 2019). Berry's integrated model for community in online courses and programs (see Figure 1.1) builds on other frameworks to highlight more contemporary experiences of students in online courses and programs. For example, the framework notes that in addition to connecting inside of virtual classrooms, students in online programs use a wide range of technology, including social and mobile media, to connect to peers (Berry, 2019). Students in online programs might create Facebook groups to connect with classmates and cohort-mates, and use mobile apps to create groups and text threads. In these groups, students can ask peers questions about assignments and give and receive encouragement. Given the role that social media plays in community formation more broadly, it is not surprising that online students find it to be an important space for creating and maintaining connections.

Berry's framework also notes that online students can and do connect offline. In some programs, online students might work with peers in-person, forming study groups on campus and in the larger community. Online students in some programs also socialize together in-person, attending sports events and participating in other group activities. This perspective on online

Figure 1.1. Berry's integrated framework for community in online courses and programs.

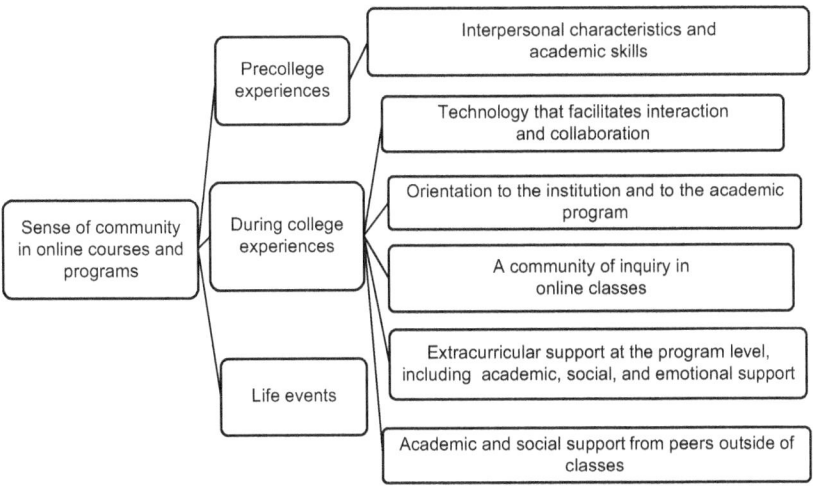

students disrupts the binary of students, even those in fully online programs, as being either fully online or fully face-to-face.

Finally, Berry's framework highlights the significance of the cocurriculum in shaping online students' experiences. Because of the binary thinking that students are either online or in-person, practitioners in online programs and scholars who research them have often failed to consider the role of the cocurriculum in supporting online students. However, research by Berry (2018a) notes that support services for online students, particularly in-person supports, can provide online students with vital connection points that can be beneficial throughout the duration of the online program. In one online program, students who met for an in-person orientation were able to build friendships with peers, even those who lived in other states. The in-person meeting was particularly helpful for Black, Indigenous, and People of Color (BIPOC) students, who were able to make connections with other Students of Color who may not have been in their courses but may have been enrolled in the same degree program. For students in some contexts, an in-person meeting, particularly when out of the state or out of the country, may not be feasible. However, some students may welcome the opportunity to travel to connect with peers. Administrators should survey their students to find out what types of in-person connections may be possible for their student body. Additionally, administrators can encourage and facilitate local and regional meet ups for online students, so that they can connect with peers that live nearby.

Cocurricular offerings for online students need not be fully online either. Hybrid and fully online services can provide vital support for distance learners. The point here is that online students need and want more support than simply classroom-based interactions. Online students benefit from the same engagement that in-person students benefit from, including academic, social, emotional, cultural, and extracurricular support.

What Is Missing From Theories of Community in Online Courses and Programs? A Need for More Inclusive Frameworks

While Berry's integrated framework for community in online courses and programs offers a more expansive framework for understanding online community, it does not explicitly engage elements related to diversity, specifically inclusion and exclusion for underrepresented and nondominant students. This is reflective of larger gaps in research on online learning. Researchers have tended to view online students as a monolith, and many scholarly articles on the topic have failed to explore in detail the experiences of diverse students, particularly as they relate to issues of race and class. As a result, there is a dearth of evidence-based practices that focus specifically on these or other areas related to diversity. This book lays the foundation for an expanded conversation about what diversity might look like in some online courses and programs. By taking an inclusive approach, researchers and practitioners can have a conversation about online teaching and learning that is at once broader and more specific to the experiences of historically marginalized and underrepresented students.

One way to do this is to move away from the term *diversity* as a catch-all term for nonwhite students. This book uses BIPOC to highlight racial/ethnic diversity. When addressing the experiences of minorities, the book uses the U.S. Department of Education's definition, which refers to *minorities* as people who are American Indian, Alaskan Native, Black (not of Hispanic origin), Hispanic (including persons of Mexican, Puerto Rican, Cuban, and Central or South American origin), and Pacific Islander.

Racial and ethnic diversity is not the only type of diversity considered in this book. In addition to considering the role of race in online learning, I consider the impact of gender, socioeconomic status, and ability and disability on the online learning experience. It is important for educators to note that these identities are not experienced separately or apart from each other. Legal theorist Kimberlé Crenshaw (1990) argues that identities can overlap, and that oppressions can overlap as well. Crenshaw uses the term *intersectionality* to note the ways in which overlapping spheres of oppression combine and constrain students' experiences in unique ways. For example, intersectionality is not just concerned with the fact that I am Black, female, and from a middle-class background; it is concerned with how racism, sexism, and classism work as interlocking forces of oppression to impact my life, constrain my choices, and cause disparate and potentially adverse outcomes in my life.

Intersectionality is a framework that is not often applied to explorations of online teaching and learning. There are many reasons why this might be the case. The overwhelming whiteness and maleness of the field of technology and online learning could be one factor. Techno-optimism about the potential of technology to bring about radical social transformation for all may be another factor. Whatever the case, I join the chorus of so many others to argue that substantive change and lasting innovation in education require honesty about the impact of racism, sexism, classism, ableism, and so many other oppressive "-isms" on the educational system. Researchers and practitioners must do more to consider the racialized experiences of BIPOC students, the gendered experiences of women and LGBTQ students, and the ableist experiences that some students with disabilities may encounter in online courses and programs. Social class is something that is also underexplored in the literature on online teaching and learning, including the experiences of low-income students, rural students, and students on tribal lands. While this discussion serves as a starting point for critical conversations in these areas, more thorough and comprehensive frameworks are needed to address the wide range of student experiences and needs. Toward that end, this work takes a broader and more inclusive lens at exploring online teaching and learning than many of the perspectives that permeate popular scholarship. This lens allows practitioners to consider the perspectives of students that are not often included in online learning.

Practitioners who seek to help all students cultivate a sense of community will be deliberate and persistent about their work around inclusion. This involves a recognition of individual and group differences, and an appreciation of similarities and differences as they relate to race/ethnicity, class, gender, sexual orientation, country of origin, religion, ability, and other identity characteristics. In an inclusive environment, the needs of historically marginalized and underrepresented people and groups are considered in every aspect of decision-making, informing both policy and practice. Further, in an inclusive environment, practitioners seek to identify and remove barriers to community, including discrimination and other forms of marginalization.

In order to move toward inclusion, practitioners must utilize equity-minded approaches. Table 1.1 provides a high-level overview of equity-minded strategies that practitioners can incorporate into teaching, leading, and planning. According to Bensimon and Malcom (2012), an equity-minded approach considers the role of race, racism, and other forms of oppression in creating and maintaining inequality, both on an interpersonal level and on a structural and systemic level. It involves directly engaging various forms of

TABLE 1.1
An Inclusive, Equity-Minded Approach to Online Teaching

1. Acknowledges that online learning is not a neutral space, and that the systematic, structural, and interpersonal oppression that is embedded in the broader society influences higher education
2. Explores how identity and identity-related oppression impact students' academic program
3. Includes the needs and experiences of underrepresented students in decision-making and planning
4. Considers structural issues that impact online learning, including access to computers and to high-speed internet
5. Recognizes the assets that underrepresented and historically marginalized students bring to higher education

inequality and their antecedents and taking a critical lens toward manifestations of inequality in policy and practice. Further, Bensimon and Malcolm (2012) note that an equity-minded approach is fundamentally data driven. Often, taking an equity-minded approach to teaching will require educators to gather their own institutional data about best practices, so that they can continually monitor what works in their unique contexts. Such a key point cannot be overlooked, even in a book like this. While strategies will be presented and considerations will be offered, the diversity of the higher education landscape means that there is no one-size-fits-all approach. It is up to the reader to engage in critical reflection and systemic inquiry around the ideas offered, and to modify them to meet their unique context. An equity-minded approach, then, has an intentional connection between reflection and action. Bensimon and Malcolm (2012) note that an equity-minded approach behooves all educational stakeholders to take action in their respective capacities to promote change. The strategies outlined in this book will help educators and administrators take action-oriented steps to creating more inclusive online communities.

It is important to note that while an equity-minded approach recognizes structural barriers created by racism and other forms of oppression, it also bears in mind that deficits are often in systems and structures, not in students. An equity-minded approach recognizes that there are many assets that historically marginalized and underrepresented learners bring to academic space and seeks to shape teaching practices and institutional policies in ways that build upon these assets.

Diversity in Online Courses and Programs

Now that diversity, equity, and inclusion have been broadly considered, it is important to explore some of the unique experiences that students from underrepresented, underserved, and historically marginalized backgrounds may encounter in online courses and programs. The sections that follow will explore the role that class, race, sex, gender, sexual orientation, and disability play in online courses and programs.

Low-Income, Rural, and Tribal Students

Online learning can present unique challenges for low-income students. Only 51% of households with incomes of $25,000 or less have desktop or laptop computers, and 59% have internet access (Ryan, 2017). These numbers increase to 86% and 89% for households with income of $50,000–$99,999 and are in the 90th percentile for households with income of over $100,000 (Ryan, 2017). Without access to the internet or computers, participating in online learning will be difficult.

Rural students and students living on tribal lands may also experience challenges with technology access. The PEW Research Center found that rural Americans have consistently lower levels of broadband adoption than Americans living in suburban or urban communities (Vogels, 2021). According to a 2019 report, 63% of rural Americans had access to home broadband, compared with 75% of Americans in urban communities and 79% in suburban communities. In addition, 69% of rural Americans reported access to a desktop or laptop computer at home, compared with 73% of urban Americans and 80% of suburban Americans. The digital divide between rural and suburban Americans reflects greater challenges in the telecommunications infrastructure. Rural adults in both higher- and lower-income households report challenges in accessing high-speed internet. In the FCC's report on broadband access, approximately 26% of rural Americans and 32% of people living on tribal lands lived in places that did not meet the minimum threshold for high-speed internet, compared to less than 2% of Americans in urban areas (FCC, 2020). Several factors contribute to the disparities in access. Rugged terrain and harsh temperatures can make building and maintaining infrastructure difficult. Internet service providers may not find it economically beneficial to offer service in areas with lower population density.

Educational institutions can do much to address these gaps. For example, institutions can offer computers and hotspots to distance learners that cannot afford them. Educators must also recognize that these interventions may still present challenges for students living in rural areas or on tribal lands, as distance and transportation issues can make it difficult to access a college campus, and terrain and infrastructure challenges can result in weak connectivity. Addressing these larger systemic issues of technology access requires collaboration between postsecondary administrators and government policymakers.

BIPOC in Online Courses and Programs

Students that have been historically marginalized in society face similar experiences of marginalization in higher education. Ribera et al., (2017) note that first-year students experience peer belonging and institutional acceptance differently based on race and ethnicity. In their nationally representative study, African American and Latinx students had a significantly lower sense of belonging than white students. For BIPOC students, feelings of belonging to an academic community can be situational and context specific. Historically marginalized students may feel included in some classes and not others. They may find some academic spaces and services (online and in person) to be supportive, while others may be hostile. Strayhorn (2012) notes that for BIPOC students, their assessments about sense of belonging are complex, and influenced by their interactions with a range of education stakeholders, including peers, faculty, and staff. Strayhorn notes that BIPOC students can have positive interactions with faculty, but feel isolated from peers, and vice versa. Guillermo-Wan et al.,(2015) add that BIPOC students' feelings of belonging and community are influenced by their perception of campus racial climate as a whole. Toward that end, administrators who wish to ensure BIPOC student success must be mindful of these students' experiences in classes, as well as their experiences on campus, with extracurricular offerings, and with support services. Additionally, administrators should consider BIPOC students racialized experiences in online classrooms. Topics that deserve further attention include racist cyberbullying of online students and faculty, faculty management of microaggressions in the online classroom, and equity and inclusion in online courses.

Another way that educators can support historically minoritized students in online programs is to implement high impact practices like learning communities, faculty research partnerships, service learning, and leadership opportunities. In face-to-face programs, these practices have been associated with increased feelings of belonging for Black and Latinx students (Ribera et al., 2017). Administrators in online programs would do well to consider which of these practices could be replicated at a distance, and what new practices could be deployed with BIPOC students' sense of belonging in mind. Administrators and staff should also consider how they can use institutional resources to support BIPOC students' unique needs as they relate to community.

Like all students, BIPOC students benefit from feelings of connection and social support. Identity-based peer networks can provide underrepresented students with an additional layer of support as well as space to receive encouragement, mentorship, and share targeted resources (Patton & Harper, 2003). These networks can be particularly important for minoritized students who are in fields or at institutions where they are particularly underrepresented. One space that has historically helped college students create and maintain these networks has been cultural centers. Black cultural centers emerged on college campuses 50 years ago, and since then, cultural centers have emerged to support other racial and ethnic groups as well. These spaces can help students with racial identity development and support students in cultivating feelings of institutional membership and belonging. Hypolite (2020) notes that cultural centers can help connect underrepresented students with campus support services. Hypolite (2020) argues that institutions can leverage the potential of support services to strategically coordinate support services for historically marginalized students. While cultural centers were initially developed to support in-person students, that does not mean they cannot support online students as well. Educators can connect online students to cultural centers and other campus supports, encouraging them to communicate with on-campus staff and find out about virtual programs that exist.

The work of supporting minoritized students goes beyond cultural centers. Educational leaders who wish to ensure that their communities are truly inclusive must also ensure that the broader campus is one that fosters a sense of belonging for all students, particularly those who are underrepresented or historically minoritized. While the role of safe spaces on campus cannot be overlooked, the racial climate of courses and classrooms as a whole plays a significant role in whether or not BIPOC students' feelings of community are supported or undermined (Hurtado et al., 2015). Faculty, staff, and administrators, including those who are not BIPOC, should be intentional about helping BIPOC students connect with networks of supportive people and services on and off campus.

BIPOC scholars are increasingly using the internet as a space where they can give and receive support to other Students of Color. There are numerous Twitter hashtags and social media profiles dedicated to amplifying the experiences of Students and Scholars of Color, and sharing resources about how to navigate the academy. Hashtags like #CiteASista, #FirstGenDocs and many others allow users to share their experiences with a global network of students from similar backgrounds. These hashtags can benefit users professionally and personally. Professionally, students might use these hashtags to connect with mentors and locate postgraduate job opportunities. Personally, students might use these hashtags to find local meet ups, including study groups and social events. Students might also use these hashtags to organize against racial injustice on specific campuses. Such digital engagement can be beneficial for BIPOC students, especially for those who are at institutions where their population is small. Instructors and administrators should encourage online students to use social media as a tool for networking, mentorship, and support.

Gender and Sex in the Online Classroom

Working, parenting, or caregiving women may be drawn to online programs for their flexibility (Berry, 2017b). Despite these benefits, online programs are not without their challenges for women. Chief among these challenges is the difficulty of balancing multiple roles. Women, even those who are involved in partnerships, may find that gendered social expectations require them to take on the lion's share of childcare or domestic work. Familial and professional obligations may add to female students' stress, even in online programs (Müller, 2008). Female students can benefit greatly from being in programs where these multiple roles are recognized, and where school leaders provide resources and support around work–life balance for women. Female students, particularly those engaged in mothering and caregiving, have found peer support from online colleagues to be helpful (Berry, 2017b; Müller, 2008). Having a sense of community can be a protective factor for these students, as it provides a space to receive support for shared challenges.

The experiences of sexual minority students specifically in online programs is a topic that is underexplored in the literature. While experiences of marginalization and harassment do not go away for these students in online courses, LGBTQ students may find the online space to provide a buffer from some of the micro and macro aggressions that occur in person. Instructors can create inclusive courses by displaying LGBTQ friendly iconography on their course pages and through virtual backgrounds, and by allowing students to utilize screen names and pronouns that reflect their gender identity.

Cyberbullying refers to "online exchanges where there is an intent to harm the recipient" (Faucher et al., 2014, p. 2). These exchanges can occur via email or via social media. While cyberbullying impacts students of all genders, it is more likely to impact women. Additionally, women are more likely to experience harassment that is often more severe, and causes greater emotional distress than the violence that men experience (Fox et al., 2015; Hess, 2017). In a survey of 1,925 Canadian university students, nearly one-quarter of female students reported experiencing cyberbullying over the course of one school year (Faucher et al., 2014). Females were more likely to experience cyberbullying by a friend or acquaintance at their university (13.6% vs. 9.4%), while males were more likely to experience cyberbullying by someone they did not know (19.3% vs.12.2%). In the study, 2% of females and 1.85% of males reported experiencing cyberbullying by a faculty member (including teaching assistants and tutors). Females cited gender as a primary reason for being cyberbullied. Victims of online harassment reported a loss of emotional security, decreased concentration and productivity, increased desire to drop out; and increased anxiety, depression, and suicidality.

The prevalence and the harms of cyberbullying suggest that faculty, administrators, and staff in online programs should take a proactive role in addressing this. In the Faucher et al. (2014) study, students suggested that universities do more to create and model a respectful culture of online student behavior, including clear anticyberbullying policies, create anonymous reporting systems for cyberbullying, quickly suspend or expel online harassers, and provide counseling and support for victims.

It is important to note that cyberbullying impacts female faculty as well. Faucher et al. (2014) found that of 1,925 Canadian university students, 5.1% said they had engaged in cyberbullying, and 2% had bullied faculty members. Students who admitted to cyberbullying said that they did so because they did not like the faculty's "teaching style," or that they found the instructor to be a "bad professor." Some respondents expressed wanting to "hurt the faculty member" and tarnish their reputation. Female scholars who experience online harassment may be harassed by students, but they might also be victimized by disgruntled internet users. In addition to the high personal costs associated with navigating online harassment, including time lost at work and legal fees, online harassment can have significant adverse impacts on female scholars' mental health.

Cyberbullying does not impact all women in the same ways. Citing Veletsianos and Kimmons (2016), Veletsianos et al. (2018) wrote that "researchers often assume that scholars' online participation is egalitarian, and often suggest that scholars' online experiences are the same regardless of race, religion, ethnic origin, ability, age, and so on" (p. 4,690). However, for female scholars who have other underrepresented identities, online harassment can be different than it is for white scholars who experience online harassment. Cottom (2015) writes about the ways in which racism and sexism influence the type of online harassment she has received as a publicly engaged scholar. Cottom reflects on how the focus of the harassment she has endured online as a Black woman has not been so much around sexual violence, but about "putting her in her place," questioning the legitimacy of her work, and suggesting that her intelligence is limited. She cites examples of other Black women scholars who have experienced harassment online, and notes that many of the attacks focus on contacting these scholars' employers to say that they have no place in the academy. Cottom (2015) notes that, like all women, Black women scholars who are cyberbullied are subject to threats of violence, but these threats also focus on harming the women at their workplace, presumably to further highlight their lack of belonging there (Cottom, 2015).

Sexual minority students also experience cyberbullying at rates that are higher than their heterosexual peers. Walker's (2015) study found that LBTQ students were more likely than their heterosexual peers to receive unwanted inappropriate and pornographic messages, have personal information shared without their consent, or have sexual behaviors and preferences outed.

Students With Disabilities in Online Courses and Programs

According to the Centers for Disease Control and Prevention (CDC), one in four adults in the United States has some type of disability (CDC, 2020). These 61 million individuals experience a wide range of disabilities, including things that impact mobility, cognition, hearing, and vision. Disabilities can also include mental, emotional, and psychiatric conditions. Postsecondary students also live with a range of disabilities. According to NCES data, 19% percent of undergraduates and 11.9% of graduate students reported having a disability (U.S. Department of Education, National Center for Education Statistics [NCES], 2021). According to the NCES, 20.8% of the undergraduate students who reported having disabilities were white, 17.2% are Black, 18.3% were Hispanic, 15.2% were Asian, 23.6% Pacific Islander, 27.8% American Indian Alaska Native. Reported disability rates were higher among veteran students than nonveteran students (25/8% vs. 19.1% for undergraduates and 17.1% vs. 11.6% for graduate students).

Students with disabilities may experience many challenges in higher education. Colleges and universities are required by federal law to ensure that facilities and to academic content be accessible to all students. However, college students still experience ableism in higher education. Examples of ableism include invasive questions about ones' disability, utilizing learning materials that are inaccessible in course sessions, assuming that people are faking disabilities because they do not appear visible, and making derogatory remarks related to disability. Instructors and administrators can support students with disabilities by ensuring that all aspects of the online program are accessible, and that accommodations are made in a swift and supportive manner. Universities should facilitate collaboration between faculty and instructional designers to ensure that course materials meet a wide range of needs.

Peña et al. (2016) note that the experience of disability is not a monolithic one. Some students may view their disability as the most prominent characteristic of their identity, and it may be the most prominent factor informing their daily experiences, including those on campus, as well as their interpersonal and extracurricular experiences. Other students might feel that other aspects of their identity are more personally salient then their disability. It is important to note that an individual's experience of their own disability may vary over time and depending on the context (Peña et al., 2016). Disability also intersects with multiple social identities including race, gender, and class, and these social categorizations can impact the perception, diagnosis, and support for people with disabilities whose identities transverse multiple categories (Mitchell, 2006; Peña et al., 2016). Because disability intersects with other identities, individuals with disabilities can experience different overlapping forms of oppression, including racism, sexism, and classism (Annamma et al., 2018).

Disability critical race theory (DisCrit) scholars encourage educators to be mindful of the ways in which matrices of oppression can intersect on college campuses, manifesting as erasure, exclusion, marginalization, and harassment of BIPOC students with disabilities. For example, using the framework of #disabilitysowhite, a social media dialogue and movement that emerged in 2016, Fovet (2020) calls out some examples of the ways in which traditional disability services might overlook BIPOC students. Examples of erasure include a lack of visual representation of BIPOC students in disability service outreach materials and a lack of nonwhite disability support professionals on certain campuses. Fovet (2020) also explores the importance of intersectional and culturally relevant disability support outreach and delivery methods. Because BIPOC and international students may have different beliefs and experiences around disability disclosure, they may not utilize support services in the same way as their white peers (Fovet, 2020). Administrators, faculty, and support staff must adopt an approach to service delivery that is culturally and contextually relevant. Additionally, scholars and practitioners have rightfully pointed out that the work of disability support is not strictly the province of disability support services. Abes and Wallace (2018) write that educators must resist manifestations of ableism in courses and classrooms by moving from accommodation to inclusion of students with disabilities. Inclusive practice requires educators to see the intersectional experiences of students with disabilities, to view students with disabilities as individuals and as members of multiple social groups, and to actively resist the ableism that permeates the dominant culture. (Abes & Wallace, 2018).

Strategies for Creating Community for Historically Marginalized and Underrepresented Students

Table 1.2 synthesizes the strategies that have emerged in this chapter. While the remainder of the book will focus on cultivating community more broadly, it is important early on to establish some of the unique needs that underrepresented and historically minoritized students have in online courses and programs, and offer suggestions for how online faculty, staff, and administrators can meet these needs. These strategies promote community in several ways. First, they ensure that all students have access to the prerequisite technologies needed to engage in learning. Second, they ensure that instructional materials and learning spaces are accessible to all students, particularly those with disabilities. Third, they ensure that courses and programs are developing experiences that promote the core characteristics of community,

TABLE 1.2
Strategies for Creating Community for Historically Marginalized and Underrepresented Students

Strategies for Promoting Community for Low-Income Students
• Ensure that all students have access to prerequisite hardware and software needed for full academic participation
• Utilize spaces like computer labs and lounges to increase on-campus access to computers and to the internet
• Make students aware of off-campus spaces where they can use internet for free or for a low cost
• Provide computers and hot spots for students in need
• Consider creating programs to help students pay for utilities or connecting students to preexisting local programs that offer such support
Strategies for Promoting Community for BIPOC Students
• Implement high-impact practices associated with increasing students' sense of belonging, including identity or affinity-based learning communities
• Create opportunities for faculty collaboration outside of the classroom, such as student-faculty research opportunities
• Connect online students to in-person support, such as cultural centers
• Develop parallel, identity-based support networks for online students
Strategies for Promoting Community for Women and Sexual Minorities
• Recognize the unique needs of students in caregiving roles
• Offer training and bystander intervention support for LGBTQIA allies
• Develop policies around clear cyberbullying, including suspension and expulsion of harassers and anonymous reporting systems for victims
Strategies for Promoting Community for Students with Disabilities
• Understand that a disability is only one aspect of a students' experience • Avoid overarching narratives of students' experiences with disability
• Ensure that faculty and staff are aware of federal and campus accessibility policies
• Ensure that teaching practices promote accessibility
• Provide faculty with training in universal design for learning and other practices that promote accessibility

including membership, belonging, trust, social support, equity, and inclusion. Finally, they reduce instances of marginalization, which are antithetical to community.

Considerations for Administrators, Instructional Designers, Faculty Developers, and Support Staff

- View online students' experiences from both the classroom level and the program level.
- Be mindful of the ways in which student support services and extracurricular experiences can impact online students. Connect online students with on-campus experiences. If no extracurricular offerings exist for online students, create them.
- Take an intersectional approach to understanding students' experiences. Regularly evaluate program components via syllabi and curriculum audits, evaluations of teaching strategy, and a review of instructional materials to ensure that courses are culturally relevant and meet the needs of a diverse set of students.
- Develop services and offerings specifically for BIPOC students and other historically minoritized students.
- Collect data on the racial climate of the online program.

Conclusion

Communities are dynamic, engaging learning spaces where students engage in shared collaboration around learning goals. Core components of community include membership, influence, fulfillment of needs, shared emotional connection, sense of belonging, and connectedness. For a classroom or program to truly become a community, equity and inclusion must be cultivated as well. The chapters that follow explore community development for all students.

2

WHAT MAKES A STRONG ONLINE INSTRUCTOR?

Creating Inclusive Communities

Online teaching is comprised of many elements. Koehler and Mishra (2009) argue that integrating technology into classes requires the presence of three distinct, but overlapping, types of knowledge—technical, pedagogical, and content knowledge. Technical knowledge refers to the knowledge and skills with using technology-related mediums. In an online course, technological knowledge would include the learning management system (LMS), the virtual classroom, and any other special software or tools to support learning. Pedagogical knowledge "deep knowledge about the processes and practices or methods of teaching and learning" (Koehler & Mishra 2009, p. 4). Pedagogical knowledge includes a general understanding of how learning occurs, and also how to support that process through classroom management, lesson planning, and assessment. Content knowledge refers to subject matter expertise in a given discipline or domain.

Of these three elements, pedagogy can be the hardest for instructors to understand, and therefore the most difficult to cultivate (Berry, 2018b). Educators and administrators may not have considered that the skills and practices needed to deliver content and engage learners differ greatly in online and face-to-face contexts. Additionally, teaching is greatly influenced by modality, temporality, and technology, among other things. Skilled online instructors will need pedagogical orientations and strategies that are rooted in the learning sciences and that are specific to synchronous, asynchronous, and hybrid contexts. Such strategies are explored in this chapter.

Social Presence—the Key to Community-Oriented Online Classes

Cultivating social presence is an important pedagogical strategy for promoting student engagement in online courses (Garrison, 2012). Social presence is about seeing peers and being seen in a virtual environment, feeling like ones' authentic identities and experiences can be brought into the classroom. When social presence is high, individuals feel like they are having genuine and meaningful interactions with others. High social presence is also associated with stronger group cohesion and a deeper sense of community (Berry, 2017a). While online researchers and practitioners have written about social presence using a broad brush, how specifically can online instructors cultivate social presence? (See Table 2.1 for strategies for cultivating social presence in online courses.)

TABLE 2.1
Strategies for Cultivating Social Presence in Online Courses

Strategy	How it Contributes to Social Presence and Sense of Community
Send an introductory video or welcome letter	Cultivates feelings of membership and belonging, increases social presence
Establish a space for students to introduce themselves	Helps students establish peer-to-peer connections and rapport
Recreate the "water cooler" by allowing a soft start to synchronous course sessions	Strengthens bonds between peers and promotes social cohesion
Encourage students to share personal and professional updates during or in between class sessions	Supports authentic sharing, increases trust and belonging
Use virtual classroom functions to promote interaction (e.g., chat, polls)	Allows for engagement by increasing the number of people who can participate in the conversation
Reach out to students often	Helps maintain community by ensuring that students are engaged, and their needs are met
Create space for ongoing collaboration in the online course	Provides space for deeper, more sustained peer engagement

Send an Introductory Video or Welcome Letter

It is important to create a warm and genuine atmosphere early on in the online class. One way to do this is to reach out to your students before the semester starts and send a welcome email. The email might include the course syllabus, and should review vital information about the course objectives and structure. The email might also include links to relevant resources and support services. However, logistics should not be the only information in the letter. A welcome letter can set the tone for the course, help manage students' expectations, and reduce feelings of distance between the student and the online instructor. Toward that end, instructors might include personal information they feel comfortable sharing that might help the students learn more about the instructor as an individual. For example, academic background, family, pets, and hobbies are common topics that could help a student get to know their instructor. Instructors who are comfortable might also consider sending pictures or a short video to introduce themselves and the course. This level of personalization can help set the tone for the learning community.

Create Space for Students to Introduce Themselves

In a face-to-face class, introductions might happen more organically. As students navigate the campus, they are likely to interact with peers, and start to learn about their colleagues informally. In the online classroom, instructors must be intentional about replicating peer-to-peer interaction. Early interactions are particularly key, as they set the tone for future interactions, by making peer dialogue the norm in the online class. Introductions early in the online course help students connect and build rapport, both of which are important for community formation and group cohesion.

There are many ways to create space for introductions. Introductions occur asynchronously, via the use of a discussion board. Rather than emailing a welcome letter, an instructor might post it to a discussion board, using it as the start of an interactive discussion thread. Using the discussion board creates space for everyone to participate and allows the introductions to be more easily organized than email. Instructors can encourage students to get creative and to share fun photos and even videos on the discussion thread. Introductions can also occur synchronously, particularly where synchronicity is already built into the program format. Allowing students to do brief introductions at the beginning of a class can go a long way toward building rapport and supporting peer interaction. Faculty who find this practice time-consuming due to large class size might use an asynchronous method to allow for preliminary introductions, and build on this in the synchronous session.

Recreate the "Water Cooler" by Allowing a Soft Start to Course Sessions

In a study of an online doctoral program, Berry (2017a) found that online students missed the water cooler conversations that occurred in face-to-face environments. The small, informal dialogue that happens in the cafeteria, coffee shop, or while students wait for courses to start can go a long way toward helping students cultivate community. Fortunately, educators can replicate the water cooler, especially in synchronous classes. Instructors might consider opening their virtual classroom a few minutes early and allowing for informal and impromptu conversation. This "soft start" will provide the space for informal conversation before the formal class session. It is in these conversations that students often learn about their peers' personal lives and extracurricular interests, which enhances their sense of connection. Instructors might start these conversations to break the ice. Common discussion topics include weather, sporting events, and popular culture. By opening the classroom early, instructors create space for peer interactions, without utilizing too much class time. In an asynchronous course, instructors can utilize discussion boards to recreate some of the water cooler experience. Instructors can encourage students to provide a weekly update or check in, and include student participation in this space as part of the course grade. To increase student engagement and provide further personalization in the asynchronous water cooler space, instructors can encourage the use of other modes of communication, such as audio or video. Regardless of the format, the opportunity to have "small talk" with peers helps facilitate student connections and contributes to online students' sense of community.

Allow Students to Share Personal and Professional Updates During Class Sessions

A core component of social presence is feeling like one is able to present their authentic self in the virtual environment. Instructors can support feelings of authenticity by allowing students to share personal and professional updates with their peers in online classes. Instructors might consider devoting a few minutes of each class to allow for this type of sharing, or, in an asynchronous course, creating a discussion board specifically for this purpose. Whatever the format, it is important that sharing is bidirectional, and students are allowed to both give and receive support from their colleagues. Creating space for students to share authentic, personal experiences leads to heightened levels of social presence and strengthens the feelings of trust and membership that are prerequisites to community. Additionally, this type of sharing can be a form of professional development for students, depending on their level. In graduate programs, sharing professional updates can provide students with valuable insight on how to navigate workplace settings and advance their careers. It can also be a form of networking, which is important, because online students have less access to informal networking opportunities.

Use Virtual Classroom Functions to Promote Interaction

Cultivating social presence requires students to talk to each other. Instructors can start a dialogue, but managing it at a distance requires special skills. To ensure that everyone can participate in a virtual dialogue, instructors should encourage the use of multiple features in the virtual classroom. Certain tools, like chat and polls, support increased participation while also streamlining discussion. For example, in the chat, all students can check in or quickly share updates. This way, each student can share, without taking too much class time. Students can also respond to their peers in the chat, allowing for increased engagement. By increasing opportunities for peer interaction, instructors support new pathways for cultivating community.

Reach Out Often to Check in With Students

It is important to check in with online students periodically to make sure that they are successfully navigating the course. This looks different depending on the course. For example, an instructor might email their students weekly or biweekly to provide a recap of the course for the week. Alternatively, an instructor might reach out to students individually over the course of the semester, checking in with them personally, soliciting feedback and providing personalized support. Additionally, an instructor might reach out and share resources that relate to the course, including resources from the campus and from the broader community. Because instructors are typically the primary link between online students and the university, sharing institutional resources is very important.

Email is not the only way to check in with students. Discussion boards can be a valuable way to maintain connections with students. An advantage of using the discussion board is that, unlike email, all students have equal access to the boards. This means that an instructor can answer a question once, instead of having to email multiple students individually. Another advantage of using the discussion board as a space to check in with students is that students and instructors can have an ongoing dialogue without getting lost in a maze of emails. Instructors might consider having different boards for different topics. For example, one board might be for personal and professional updates, another board can be for questions about reading, and another board can be about questions for upcoming assignments. Organizing boards by topic can help students and instructors easily navigate them. However, instructors who use discussion boards in this way must make sure that they monitor them and quickly respond to student concerns.

Create Space for Collaboration in the Online Class

Collaboration, which requires working together to develop shared meaning, has many benefits for learners. It provides an opportunity for students to exchange ideas with peers, which enhances learning. Additionally, some students are more likely to express themselves in smaller, collaborative groups, producing a deeper quality of interaction between peers. Collaboration also has benefits for postgraduate outcomes. Group work can help students develop leadership and project management skills, and learn how to build consensus and resolve conflict. As employers are increasingly utilizing location-independent and diverse teams, these skills will be highly beneficial in the labor market.

While some online students prefer working independently, many indicate that collaborative activities with peers can increase students' sense of community (Athens, 2018; Berry, 2017a). Collaborative activities require dialogue, a necessary prerequisite for connection and community. Additionally, the exchange of ideas can stimulate cognitive presence, a key facilitator of community. Collaborative activities also heighten social presence, as students might work with each other through chatting, social media, or other mediums that promote a deeper, more personal way of interacting.

What Makes a Strong Collaborative Task?

In an online class, collaboration can occur in many forms. Instructors can create virtual spaces for collaboration (e.g., breakout rooms). They can also encourage the use of collaborative documents (eg., Google Docs) or create shared workspaces for collaboration (e.g, virtual whiteboards). Instructors can also facilitate collaborative activities in a whole group session, including think-pair-share, fishbowl, case-study analysis, task-oriented problem solving, project development and management, group assessments, and creative collaborations. Before exploring these activities in more detail, it is helpful to consider what makes a strong collaborative task. A strong collaborative task is one that

- is relevant to the course learning outcomes and overall assessment
- is understandable, but rigorous, and students should be able to complete the task with limited support, but still find a challenge
- allows students with enough direction to achieve a shared goal, but flexible enough to encourage creativity—instructions that are too didactic might limit critical thinking and stifle student engagement
- spans the range of Bloom's taxonomy—tasks that focus on the lowest aspect of the taxonomy, remembering, don't take advantage of the depth of learning that collaboration affords; consider tasks that allow students to create, evaluate, and analyze
- relates to students' broader interests within and beyond the course—projects that connect to "the real world" are likely to boost engagement and strengthen participation

Instructors should consider allowing students to have creative control over some aspect of the collaborative assignment. Instructors might consider allowing students multiple ways to demonstrate task mastery, including determining what the summative output looks like. Instructors can also encourage creativity by allowing students to bring in a variety of resources for the project, including those from outside of the course. When instructors give students choice in the decision-making process, they can learn more about the teaching strategies, processes, and instructional materials that best meet students' needs.

As with all learning activities, collaborative tasks should be relevant to course learning outcomes and to students' needs. Students will deem activities as superfluous or engage in them begrudgingly if they are not clearly connected to the learning objectives for the course. One way to demonstrate the alignment between the activities and the course content is to make sure that collaboration is reflected in the overall assessment for the course, that is, the course grade. Typically, if students know that they will be graded for their work with peers, they will be more likely to fully participate. At the same time, instructors should be mindful of assigning too much weight to collaborative work, particularly in online classes. A strong online class should encourage collaborative activities, but have many opportunities for independent assessment as well. (See Table 2.2 for collaborative activities that support community.)

TABLE 2.2
Collaborative Activities That Support Community

Activity	Description	Relationship to Community
Peer Facilitation	In synchronous courses, students can facilitate a portion of the class. Students can teach lessons, moderate discussions, and guide learning activities. In asynchronous courses, students can moderate discussion boards and give feedback on peer assignments.	Having students serve as facilitators increases their engagement with course material. As students give and receive feedback to their peers, they develop feelings of trust and belonging. Having students work collaboratively to facilitate, helps students develop teamwork skills, which in turn influence students' sense of community.
Creating a Shared Resource	In some courses, especially those with a social justice orientation or a field-based component, instructors might encourage students to share what they have learned with the broader community. One way to do that is to create a shared resource. Students might create zines, websites, handouts, videos, or other forms of media to share their knowledge.	Creating a shared resource allows students to connect with each other, and with the broader community. By engaging in shared meaning-making, students can develop bonds that contribute to their sense of community.
Program Evaluation	Students can use evaluation techniques to evaluate a program, product, process, or service. Depending on the topic of the evaluation, students can engage in collaboration remotely, working at a distance to collect and analyze data.	Program evaluation requires a high degree of coordination and project management. Collaborating in this way can promote social cohesion, which influences students' sense of community.

Serving Historically Marginalized and Underrepresented Students: Safety as the Foundation for Community

The aforementioned steps create a foundation for deeper social presence in online classrooms and offer a starting point for community. However, instructors who wish to create inclusive and engaging communities for all students, including those that have been historically marginalized, will need to go a step further. Safety is a prerequisite for online community. Feelings of safety reduce the likelihood that instances of marginalization, including microaggressions or more overt discrimination will occur. If they do occur, feelings of safety increase the likelihood that the affected student(s) will receive redress. Also, safety provides the foundation for feelings of trust, which helps cultivate community.

Creating a Safe Environment for All Students

Broadly speaking, safety in an online course can be supported by establishing clear guidelines for participation in the online course. This includes establishing norms for how students should engage with the content and with peers. Even guidelines that seem simple, such as making explicit how to speak and to listen in the online course, how to take turns communicating, and how to give and receive feedback might promote feelings of safety for students, especially those who are more likely to be ignored or marginalized in academic settings.

Beyond general guidelines regarding class participation, instructors can help underrepresented students feel safer in the classroom by being explicit about what type of communication is not acceptable in the course. Instructors who make clear that racist, sexist, homophobic, ableist, or otherwise discriminatory participation will not be tolerated can signal to students from historically marginalized underrepresented backgrounds that the classroom is a safe space for them.

To make classrooms feel safer for all participants, particularly those that are trans, nonbinary, or gender nonconforming, instructors should be careful to not make assumptions around students' gender. One concrete way faculty can do this is to utilize and model gender inclusive language. Rather than using statements like, "ladies and gentlemen," terms like "folks" or "everyone" ensure that the class is more inclusive of students who are transgender and nonbinary, as well as students who wish to not be gendered. Instructors should allow each student to begin the term by sharing their name and pronouns. Instructors can also allow students to introduce themselves via an information sheet. This way, in the event that a students' name does not reflect what is listed on an official roster, the student has an opportunity to share their name and pronouns without being "dead named." Deadnaming, or the practice of using a name that does not align with one's chosen or affirmed name can create anxiety and stress for transgender and nonbinary individuals.

Supporting Safety and Inclusion: Conduct an Equity Audit of Your Syllabi

The University of Southern California's Center for Urban Education (CUE, 2020) notes that syllabi can be a way for faculty to demonstrate equity-mindedness. Through syllabi, faculty can demonstrate their commitment to equity and inclusion through statements that outline what they value, course materials that support a wide range of perspectives, including those from historically minoritized populations, and through assignments that promote critical reflection.

CUE (2020) recommends six steps for an equity-minded syllabus:

1. welcoming students
2. demystifying college policies and practices
3. having concrete examples of what partnership between faculty and students looks like
4. validating students' ability to be successful
5. representing a range of racial/ethnic experiences in coursework
6. decentering whiteness as the normative standard of learning and of success

The syllabus is a starting point for creating a more inclusive classroom, but it is not an ending point. Another way to signal safety and create conditions for equity and inclusion is to utilize course materials that reflect a range of experiences and perspectives. Instructors who are committed to equity and social justice should ensure that their course materials reflect a broad range of cultural and philosophical perspectives. It is particularly important for instructors to incorporate content that is not just about—but is created by—people who are from historically marginalized and underrepresented backgrounds. Including course materials written and developed by women, BIPOC, persons with disabilities, and LGBTQ persons increases the likelihood that underrepresented students will feel represented by and included in course curriculum. In turn, these students will be more likely to feel like the classroom is a safe space where they can share more of themselves and be embraced by the classroom community.

Beyond Safety: Moving Toward Inclusion

Once safety is promoted, instructors can move toward inclusion. By purposefully creating classrooms centered on the needs of all students, online instructors, staff, and administrators can make more inclusive online courses and programs.

Supporting Inclusion for Students With Disabilities

Promote inclusion for students with disabilities by affirming the diversity of disability. Not making assumptions, including the assumption that disabilities will be rendered visible. Another way to support students with disabilities is by incorporating frameworks that optimize learning, like universal design for learning (UDL) in the course. UDL is beneficial for disabled and non-disabled students alike. UDL encourages the use of teaching tools, strategies, and practices that allow for multiple means of representation, expression, and engagement as a way to create greater accessibility and inclusion for all learners. For example, some UDL strategies in the college classroom might include

- adding closed captioning to recorded videos
- ensuring that course materials can be easily read by screen readers
- presenting content in different forms (written, oral, visual)
- providing visual representations for complex concepts

According to the Higher Education Opportunity Act of 2008, UDL "reduces barriers in instruction, provides appropriate accommodations, supports, and challenges, and maintains high achievement expectations for all students, including students with disabilities and students who are limited English proficient" (U.S. Department of Education, 2008, sec. 103). In this way, UDL removes barriers to community and ensures that all students can fully participate.

The perceivable, operable, understandable, and robust (POUR) framework outlined in chapter 3 (this volume) also provides more comprehensive examples of accessible teaching strategies. Additionally, educators who are looking for more research on UDL techniques and strategies might explore the work of the Center for Applied Special Technology (CAST). CAST developed UDL, and they currently conduct research and provide resources about how to implement UDL. Instructional designers and faculty developers can also provide support in this area.

Supporting Inclusion for Women, LGBTQIA, and Nonbinary Students

Gender-affirming classes support women, nonbinary, and sexual minority students. Gender-affirming classrooms are spaces where students and instructors recognize the diversity of gender identity and expression as extending beyond a binary. Wheaton College's (2020) website notes that "Making a classroom gender-affirming goes beyond pronouns; it also plays out in the texts we assign and the ways we discuss them" (para. 9). They recommend acknowledging exclusionary and heteronormative language when it occurs in course content, and encouraging critical reflection when course texts reflect outdated assumptions about sex, gender, and gender roles. Instructors should acknowledge the underlying assumptions of course content, and support students in critically interrogating it. Instructors should also strive to include work in their courses from diverse creators, including women, LGBTQIA people, and queer and nonbinary thinkers.

Supporting Inclusion for BIPOC Students: Antiracism and the Online Classroom

Antiracist pedagogy seeks to actively confront individual and structural racism and to institutions and society in more just and equitable ways (Blakeney, 2005). There is no one way to demonstrate antiracism. Instead, it is about a commitment to continuous reflection about how power and privilege have shaped society and a commitment to disrupting policies and practices that oppress certain groups of people (Kendi, 2019). Antiracist pedagogy has received renewed attention over the past decade, and gained even greater recognition in the year 2020 following the murder of an unarmed Black man, George Floyd, by Minneapolis police. Floyd's murder sparked nationwide protests and civil unrest in some cities. That summer, many colleges and universities issued statements on racial justice and antiracism. EAB, a research and consulting firm, analyzed 130 such statements from U.S. and Canadian institutions. These statements included a renewed commitment to diversity, equity and inclusion (DEI) research, data collection on instances of marginalization and harassment on campus, and DEI training for students, faculty, and staff. However, few institutions have put forth an agenda for what antiracist teaching looks like at their institutions. While many educators have shared antiracist content over the internet, including books like Ibram Kendi's (2019) *How to Be an Antiracist* and Robin DiAngelo's (2018) *White Fragility*, few have considered what an antiracist pedagogy looks like specifically as it relates to online teaching and learning.

In order for a classroom to truly be inclusive, educators must be committed to removing barriers that would seek to exclude and marginalize members of nondominant groups. Often, these barriers are embedded in our curriculum, as well as the practices of our respective disciplines and fields. Educators can empower students by helping them reflect on the silent norms and biases of their areas of study. Collaborative and reflective assignments on power and privilege in a particular area of study strengthen students' ability to recognize inequality in society more broadly. While these activities can be difficult for some, they can also promote greater reflection, authenticity, and transparency, which will support students' sense of community. For BIPOC students, an analysis of oppression, power, and privilege can create greater space for their experiences to be acknowledged in the classroom. For white students, these types of discussions can give them language to analyze social conditions more broadly and provide them with the tools to fight for social transformation. In such an environment, all students can cultivate feelings of connection and community.

Learning Activities That Support DEI

Writing activities can be used to help students cultivate skills of self-disclosure. After faculty build students' capacity for authentic reflection and sharing, as well as their skills in deep listening and cultural awareness, they might transition to partnered discussions as a way to promote sustained reflection and collaboration around social justice (Ukpokodu, 2008). Additionally, faculty can implement larger collaborative activities as a way for students to reflect on DEI in their online classes and to develop a sense of community. Project-based learning (PBL) and action research are two applied teaching techniques that online instructors can use to help students build their capacity for inclusion and also help cultivate community.

PBL is a teaching approach that begins with a pressing question or problem and allows students to respond creatively to that question (Lee et al., 2014). PBL privileges meaningful learning activities over rote or scripted activities. PBL also encourages the public presentation of the project, its findings, and community implications. PBL presentations can be more traditional symposia or discussion forms, or more creative, including the creation of performances, art displays, booklets, zines, or other types of art. PBL activities often have a strong social justice component, making them appropriate for educators who want to help students develop a deeper sense of DEI. Educators can have students engage in products that raise awareness about social issues as well as projects that promote social change.

There are many benefits to PBL (Larmer & Mergendoller, 2010). It provides students with an opportunity for shared responsibility. Additionally, PBL tends to give students greater creative authority. The personalization that PBL affords can lead to more opportunities for self-disclosure and provide peers with opportunities to identify shared personal and professional interests. This type of sharing can help students cultivate a deeper level of peer-to-peer awareness and trust. In these ways, PBL helps students cultivate a sense of community.

Action research is a research methodology and teaching approach that can be transformative for students (Stringer, 2008). Action research is a cyclical process that involves continuous research, reflection, and action. In a typical action research arc, a researcher begins with a problem, develops a plan to respond to the problem, implements the plan, observes the implementation and outcomes, and evaluates the effectiveness of the plan. Action research is iterative, meaning that practitioners can go through several cycles of implementation, reflection, and action. Because action research is concerned with reducing the time between implementation and action, it is well-suited to support teaching and learning around areas of DEI. Students can create social justice and social change-oriented programs, policies and practices, and gain immediate feedback on their impact.

Like PBL, action research can help students cultivate community. Action research provides students with an opportunity to connect their learning to issues that are personally meaningful. Additionally, the full action learning cycle means that an outcome is produced at the end. For some students, the opportunity to see tangible results from learning can provide a deeper connection to the curriculum and to their peers. The project management required by action research also provides students with opportunities to manage group dynamics and creates an opportunity for deeper bonds to form. Finally, action research projects tend to have immediate impact on the broader community. Working collaboratively with peers to make a positive change in a broader community can help students feel closer to each other, even at a distance. Action research, then, can be a powerful catalyst for community.

What Makes a Strong Online Instructor?

At minimum, a strong online instructor will be able to cultivate community through

- strong content knowledge
- strong technical knowledge
- an awareness of online pedagogy, and what it means to teach with technology and use that technology to cultivate content knowledge in a particular field of study

Additionally, a strong online instructor will

- implement practices that help students develop a greater sense of social presence
- encourage peer-to-peer collaboration and authentic sharing

A strong online instructor will also be intentional at making the online classroom safe and inclusive for students of historically marginalized and underrepresented backgrounds. Some of the strategies outlined in this chapter include:

- implementing UDL and other frameworks to ensure coursework and instruction are accessible to all students
- utilizing gender-inclusive language
- critically interrogating norms in the field
- directly engaging topics of power and privilege in course learning activities
- demonstrating a commitment to antiracism through tangible expressions of allyship and through incorporating explorations of race and racism into course content
- utilizing active learning techniques like PBL and action research to promote collaboration and reflection around DEI

Considerations for Administrators

This chapter helps administrators understand the core components of an online course. As Koehler and Mishra (2009) note, online instruction requires technical, pedagogical, and content knowledge. Institutions often lean heavily into technical knowledge, focusing on the nuts and bolts of LMSs, but may overlook the intricacies of online pedagogy, and discipline-specific online pedagogy. Administrators might use this heuristic to assess the professional development they provide, exploring whether it provides support for both the cultivation of these three elements independently, and their skillful integration in the online class.

The COI framework allows educators to delve deeper into what high-quality online pedagogy looks like, including elements like social presence, which is often overlooked, even though it is the lifeblood of an online community. The chapter provides best practices around social presence and provides administrators with an opportunity to use these practices as norms for their online courses and programs. Administrators should also consider how they might observe, encourage, and reward faculty efforts to promote social presence in online classes.

This chapter provides tangible ways for faculty to create more inclusive online courses. Administrators should take note of the strategies recommended for supporting BIPOC students, LGBTQ students, and students with disabilities. Additionally, school leaders should provide training, support, incentives, and other resources to prepare faculty to do this work. Administrators might also reflect on how they can incentivize faculty participation in equity-oriented teaching. Devoting attention to exemplary faculty who are seeking to model their teaching practice for others is one way to build an equity-minded campus culture.

Hopefully, the ideas outlined in this chapter encourage educators to become more reflective of the specific equity and inclusion challenges that confront their institution. The ideas provided here are a starting point and should be built upon to meet institution specific needs. It is important to note that administrators need not develop these best practices alone or in a silo. Collaborating with faculty and students in this area can be quite beneficial in ensuring that the practices developed actually meet the needs of your population. Administrators should consider creating space for such collaborations to occur, both through the provision of time and through the allocation of financial resources for collaboration.

Education leaders looking to make long-term change would do well to consider how they might institutionalize some of these strategies and practices, both by connecting them directly to teaching and learning, and by creating accountability measures and metrics. While institutions have implemented a wide swath of reform efforts aimed at DEI, ranging from resource pages on antiracist teaching, institutional and unit level plans, and research centers to explore race and racism in the broader society, these efforts may or may not be explicitly connected to teaching and learning. Administrators seeking to advance DEI initiatives at their institutions should utilize systemic plans for assessing knowledge development and evidence of instructional implementation and change.

Considerations for Instructional Designers, Faculty Developers, and Other Staff in Centers for Teaching and Learning

This chapter highlights the complexities associated with strong online teaching. It involves teaching and facilitation techniques, as well as the use of transformative and inclusive pedagogies. It also involves understanding the fundamentals of strong online teaching. When faculty recognize that online teaching is informed by technical, pedagogical, and content knowledge, they can be better positioned to utilize the services that can help develop these different elements of knowledge. For example, instructional design teams can assist with many elements of technology. Beyond basic technical support, instructional designers are uniquely positioned to help faculty reflect on universal design and accessibility, two important elements of a more inclusive online classroom. Faculty developers can be able to provide support around teaching strategies that promote a COI, and can provide more targeted, institution and context-specific strategies to cultivating teaching presence, social presence, and cognitive presence.

This chapter also highlights the importance of high-quality facilitation in online teaching. Instructors must know how to engage students academically and personally. Instructors and administrators might work with instructional designers, faculty developers, and staff in centers for teaching and learning to create opportunities for deep and authentic student engagement. This chapter also highlights areas for faculty development that staff in centers for teaching and learning should consider offering, if they do not already. Faculty who are seeking to create antiracist, gender affirming, and accessible classrooms may rightly turn to centers for teaching and learning for support. Support staff might guide faculty in reflecting on their own power and privilege, and how it impacts their course design and facilitation. Faculty support staff can lead faculty on an audit of their own courses, asking them to analyze their syllabi through an equity-oriented lens. In certain contexts, this work might also involve educating administrators on the importance of transformational teaching, and provide them with examples of what it might look like. In these ways, support staff can shift the culture of institutions. The center for teaching and learning (CTL) staff can also shift institutional culture by working with faculty and administrators to develop norms, goals, and short-term and long-term plans in these areas to ensure that diversity work is monitored, measured, and institutionalized.

Conclusion

A strong online instructor will implement a wide range of strategies to promote social presence. By creating multiple opportunities for students to learn about peers personal and professional interests, online instructors lay a foundation for feelings of membership, trust, and belonging to occur. Instructors can build on this foundation by trying to create communities that are inclusive of all students. Instructors can demonstrate a commitment to DEI by using instructional practices that recognize and affirm all students. This chapter highlights many of the foundational elements of strong online teaching, and by extension, robust online communities. Chapter 3 (this volume) delves deeper into this area, highlighting the ways in which technology can be leveraged to facilitate connections and support community.

3

THE ROLE OF TECHNOLOGY IN THE ONLINE CLASSROOM

It can be easy to think of online courses as duplicates of their in-person counterparts. While instructors might set out to re-create their face-to-face courses in distance formats, they often learn that the two environments are different, and require different approaches to course design. Bower (2008) and others have argued that different technologies provide different affordances, or educational and social opportunities for teaching, learning, and connecting. As such, online courses cannot be viewed as simple parallels to face-to-face courses, but unique experiences that provide distinct opportunities for community and connection. Nor can they be viewed as a monolith. The temporal design of the course plays a role in the way instructors teach and students learn. This chapter explores the opportunities for learning that synchronous, asynchronous, and hybrid courses offer for creating community. This chapter also considers the role of the LMS and the virtual classroom in supporting community, as well as considerations for equity in selecting course delivery methods and educational tools for the online class.

Synchronous, Asynchronous, and Hybrid Learning: The Role of Temporality in Online Courses

Online courses can either be asynchronous, synchronous, or hybrid. In an asynchronous course, students do not attend class simultaneously. Rather, they complete learning activities independently, typically within a preestablished window. In a synchronous course, students meet at an established time, typically through a Web conferencing system or virtual classroom. Hybrid courses, also called blended courses, include a combination of synchronous and asynchronous teaching. The synchronous facets of a hybrid course can be online or in-person. The following sections will explore the educational and social opportunities provided by different modes of learning.

Asynchronous Learning

Because asynchronous courses do not occur in real time, students have greater flexibility over when they complete course assignments. While flexibility is a key function of an asynchronous course, they are not totally self-paced. Asynchronous courses often have deadlines embedded in them, both for when the entire course is to be completed, as well as for when specific assignments are due. Due dates can encourage student accountability, and also allow instructors to provide feedback on student work. Additionally, there should be due dates for activities that require peer interaction, such as discussion boards.

In the early days of distance learning, asynchronous courses, or correspondence courses, occurred through the mail. Presently, many asynchronous courses are facilitated through an LMS. Using the LMS, an instructor will typically post content for students to engage with. The instructor may also ask the students to submit written assignments in response to the course content. Asynchronous courses can also include reflective assignments, projects, and exams. Asynchronous courses can provide students with greater independence over their learning, but they can include collaborative activities as well. Discussion boards, which have become a mainstay of asynchronous courses, allow for peer-to-peer interaction and can contribute to students' sense of community in an asynchronous environment.

Strengths of Asynchronous Courses

One of the main attractions of asynchronous courses is the flexibility they offer. Because they are neither location nor time-bound, asynchronous courses can be completed from virtually anywhere. For students with intense professional or personal demands, this flexibility can be attractive. Asynchronous courses can also offer flexibility for how students learn. In a self-guided asynchronous course, students can create unique timelines around when to complete course content. Even in an instructor-led course, students still have a relatively high degree of flexibility over when they complete their course work, which can be beneficial for some learners. For struggling students, this flexibility can allow them the opportunity to seek additional support for learning. For advanced students, the flexible pace can allow them to complete the course quickly, creating more time for personal and professional goals.

In a study of over 1,000 Chinese undergraduate students, Lin and Gao (2020) found that self-directed learning was a benefit of asynchronous course structure. Students appreciated the ability to start and stop a video lecture. Students also expressed motivation toward creative, independent problem solving. Students also found the flexibility and efficiency of this type of learning to be beneficial. Even in courses that are not fully asynchronous, the use of asynchronous materials in courses also can help students connect with courses more deeply. Opportunities to start and stop prerecorded videos and to watch them multiple times can help strengthen students' comprehension.

Considerations for Asynchronous Courses

One challenge students can experience in asynchronous courses is the difficulty of peer-to-peer interaction. Depending on their design, asynchronous courses can provide limited opportunities for communication and collaboration, leading to increased feelings of social isolation. In Lin and Gao's (2020) study, students lamented the lack of opportunities to interact with peers and to benchmark their progress against their colleagues. Even when instructors intentionally embed interactive activities into asynchronous courses, students can feel disconnected, due to the delay in response times. The inherent lag in asynchronous communication can be difficult for some students to manage, and can increase feelings of disconnection from the learning community. Strategies for promoting connection in asynchronous courses are outlined in chapter 4 (this volume).

Synchronous Learning

Synchronous courses occur in real time. Some blended programs have a face-to-face component which accounts for their synchronous time. Other courses use the term *synchronous* to refer to online courses or course sessions that meet online, synchronously. For the purpose of this book, the later definition is used. The structure of synchronous courses varies, but typically participants utilize some type of Web conferencing system (e.g. Zoom, WebEx, Elluminate Live) to connect via audio. A growing number of online programs are encouraging or requiring the use of video to participate in synchronous courses.

Strengths of Synchronous Courses

An attractive feature of synchronous courses is that they provide students with an immediate space to connect with instructors and peers. This immediacy is associated with deeper feelings of membership, belonging, and trust, which are prerequisites for community. Immediacy can be heightened by the multiple features of a virtual classroom, including the use of video, chat, and breakout rooms.

Considerations for Synchronous Courses

Like asynchronous courses, a strength of synchronous courses is that they are not place-bound. However, unlike asynchronous courses, they are time-bound, and this might place constraints on student participation. For students who lack access to consistent, stable, or high-speed internet, synchronicity might be difficult. Martin and Bollinger (2018) found that students rated synchronous classrooms as either the most or least helpful facet of their online learning experience. Some students in their survey felt that the group discussions in real time enhanced their learning and stimulated their engagement, while others found the time commitment to be burdensome. McDaniels et al., (2016) similarly found mixed reviews of synchronous learning. They found that some students enjoyed being able to communicate simultaneously through talk and text, while others struggled with managing multiple communication features at the same time. Berry (2017b) found that instructors must be skilled in using synchronous platforms in ways that engage but do not overwhelm students. Strategies for maximizing the technical facets of an online classroom and using them to build community are included in the sections that follow.

Blended and Hybrid Formats

Joyner et al. (2020) have written about a synchronicity paradox, which is the idea that online students want the sense of community that synchronicity affords, while also desiring the flexibility that asynchronicity affords. For this reason, a blended format might be beneficial for students. The balance of independent work and synchronous meetings might provide students with a helpful balance of flexibility and accountability. Students can work independently during asynchronous times, and then gain clarification and support for academic work during synchronous sessions. Yamagata-Lynch (2014) found that the blended format helped learners stay on task in an academic program.

The strength of a blended program is that it offers what some students might describe as "the best of both worlds." Students are able to work independently as they need, but also gain peer and instructor support in real time. The synchronous sessions of a blended program also provide students with opportunities to establish social connections, which they can build on independently as they choose. This combination of engagement and independence can have positive impacts on students' sense of community, particularly for students who are proactive about seeking social, emotional, and academic support. However, students who struggle with connecting asynchronously may feel overwhelmed and adrift in a blended program, especially if they are unsure of how to engage with peers and colleagues between sessions.

Instructors teaching in blended courses should be mindful of the potential for an increased workload, both for faculty and for students. Additionally, some blended course instructors struggle with fully integrating synchronous and asynchronous course components. If synchronous and asynchronous elements are not intentionally integrated, students will feel like they are in two separate courses, instead of a course where the learning activities and experiences are blended into one seamless, manageable course. Instructors should be mindful that a blended course does not result in a workload for students that is double that of a synchronous, asynchronous, or in-person course. While some instructors struggle with including too much into a blended course, other instructors struggle with incorporating too little into a blended course. Content in blended courses can become repetitive, especially if synchronous sessions function as mere recaps of asynchronous content. In selecting learning activities and experiences for a blended classroom, instructors should consider the unique opportunities of synchronous and asynchronous learning and try to maximize the affordances of both.

Temporality and Community

Asynchronous, synchronous, and blended courses impact students' sense of community in different ways. In synchronous courses, the opportunity to regularly see classmates and instructors heightens feelings of immediacy and intimacy. Synchronicity provides students with the opportunity to develop their relationships with their peers over time, sharing more as the term unfolds. Asynchronous courses also allow for peer-to-peer sharing, however, this is not necessarily endemic to the format. Unless instructors intentionally develop community-building activities into asynchronous

TABLE 3.1
Strengths of Various Online Formats

Format	Asynchronous	Synchronous	Hybrid/Blended
Learning Opportunities	Typically requires lower bandwidth, making the option more accessible to students with limited internet access. Offers flexibility to students, as they can complete assignments from anywhere. Provides learners with the ability to review course materials at their own pace. For some students, this can allow them to complete coursework more quickly. For students needing additional academic support, asynchronous learning provides time to review content multiple times, and at a slower pace.	The combination of live audio and visual elements can enhance feelings of social presence. Students can receive instant support from instructors and make immediate connections with peers, increasing their engagement in the course.	For some students, hybrid learning can feel like "the best of both worlds," as the synchronous component can provide a space for accountability and an opportunity for community maintenance, while the asynchronous component can provide learners with flexibility and autonomy.

courses, deep connections between peers can be difficult for students to develop. Blended and hybrid course formats can be beneficial in that they offer the best of both worlds. In a blended format, synchronous learning offers a space for significant initial community-building, while asynchronous learning gives students autonomy over how they will connect with peers and instructors.

Choosing a Mode of Instruction in a Time of Crisis

Synchronous instruction poses some challenges in an emergency context like a natural disaster or pandemic. There is the issue of time, as some online students are in time zones that differ from the home institution and from peers. There is also the issue of access, as newly displaced students may have variable access to the internet and even to computers. Additionally, internet access can become more constrained during certain crises. Certain disasters can overload impact telecommunication systems. As the COVID-19 pandemic forced states to establish shelter in place orders, some students found that their internet bandwidth was limited as they were forced to share WiFi with family members who were also working and attending school. These and other challenges associated with learning through a crisis can make synchronous learning difficult in emergency situations.

At the same time, for those institutions that can help students successfully manage the challenges associated with scheduling and technology access, synchronous learning can be beneficial for students, particularly in times of crisis. For example, Lowenthal et al., (2020) found that synchronous online learning during the COVID-19 pandemic helped students maintain a sense of community. Students found the opportunity to have regular class meetings during an unsettling time provided them with a sense of consistency and closeness. Students appreciated the opportunity to regularly receive and give emotional support to their peers.

While synchronous learning has its benefits, instructors might consider a blended format, or even heavily asynchronous format during an emergency situation. An asynchronous format might increase the likelihood that more students actually have access to the course, and are able to engage with it in a way that best meets their needs. Students may find it easier to navigate internet access and connection issues asynchronously. Additionally, the flexibility that asynchronous learning provides might align better with schedules that may have shifted due to a crisis. However, instructors should be aware that a sudden shift to asynchronous learning can result in lost connection points for students as well as reduced opportunities for community-building. Educators should consult with their students to develop a format for emergency remote teaching that meets their needs.

The Unique Nature of the Online Environment: Inside the LMS and Virtual Classroom

Today, most institutions rely on a LMS to deliver online courses. An LMS is an integrated Web platform which houses the collaboration tools used for course content (e.g., message boards and video conferencing systems), as well as student management tools (e.g., grades, rosters, and course calendars). Instructors can use LMSs to teach classes, administer tests, store data, and communicate with students. Popular LMSs include Instructure (Canvas), D2L, Blackboard, and Moodle.

LMSs have three core functions:

- *pedagogical functions*—create and administer learning activities (discussion boards, quizzes, presentation tools, assignments, etc.)
- *communication functions*—facilitate communication between instructor and a course, instructor, and individual students; and in some cases, peer-to-peer
- *productivity functions*—help instructors manage submissions of student work, manage grade book, and create an overall assessment profile of individual students

The different functions of an LMS allow it to support learning in many ways. First, they allow for one central location to store course content. This makes it easy for individual users, and also makes it possible for institutions to copy courses from instructor-to-instructor or from year-to-year. Second, they allow content to be modified remotely and accessed remotely. This offers a benefit to both instructors and students, who can teach and learn from any location. Third, they offer an easy way for an instructor to facilitate learning activities; including exams, discussions, and other assignments.

Another benefit of an LMS is that it can help instructors and institutions capture student learning data, which can in turn influence course development and learner support. One type of data that an LMS collects is usage data, which is information about how frequently students use particular aspects of a course. This might include log in data, clicks on a link, file downloads, or time spent on a page. In addition to using this information to learn about individual students, instructors can use this information to make decisions about the course as a whole. Instructors might consider what types of resources students engage with more frequently, and what the relationship is between using particular materials and successfully completing a course. Another type of data an LMS collects is achievement data. Instructors can easily organize information about student performance on assignments, and use this data to identify students who need additional assistance. All of these data points can be used by instructors to identify struggling students. Sometimes, academic challenges can indicate other challenges, including social and psychological adjustment difficulties. Instructors might reach out to students who are struggling and provide them with more targeted support for connecting to the learning community.

Learning and Community-Building Opportunities Provided by Asynchronous Tools

Asynchronous content can be accessed on demand. The affordances of two widely used asynchronous tools for online teaching, asynchronous discussion boards, and asynchronous videos are reviewed in this section.

Discussion Boards

Discussion boards are a common component of asynchronous teaching and learning. In an online discussion board, sometimes called a forum, participants can post messages and comment on them. Discussion boards offer several unique benefits to learners. They allow participants to have an in-depth conversation over an extended period of time. Because they are asynchronous, participants can reflect on their responses, allowing for more thoughtful and deliberate commentary. Some students, including those who have difficulty speaking in large groups or quickly organizing their thoughts will appreciate the added time for reflection and expression. In some ways, the discussion board can be a more equitable way to ensure class participation, as all students have space to participate. When done correctly, discussions can increase students' sense of community.

While discussion boards can offer opportunities for more deliberate reflection, it is important to note that this does not always occur. Some instructors have lamented the limited, passive participation that can occur in discussion forums. Such participation includes surface level responses, preoccupation with word count, not bridging theory and practice, and avoiding authentic peer engagement (Petty & Farinde, 2013; Zyngier, 2008). Another challenge of asynchronous discussions is that students might disengage from them prematurely. Reasons for disengagement include gaps in response time, and limited or nonexistent feedback from instructors and peers. Strategies for developing more engaging discussion boards are outlined in chapter 4 (this volume).

Asynchronous Video

Asynchronous videos can help support a dynamic and engaging online course. Instructors can share video from YouTube and other online sources.

They can also create videos for their courses. Customized videos can be used to welcome students, explain assignments, or review course content. Personalized video content creates deeper social presence and supports online students' sense of community.

Asynchronous videos are also a great learning support. One opportunity video provides students with is the chance to engage with course material at their own pace. Students can pause, forward, and rewind video. Students can also watch videos as often as needed. Videos can be close-captioned, providing vital support for students with disabilities as well as for international students, English language learners, and nonnative-English speakers. The use of video in online class has been associated with deeper understanding of course content (Ozan & Ozarslan, 2016).

A growing number of mobile applications for asynchronous video allow users to create ongoing video conversations. Tools like Edconnect and Flipgrid allow users to post a video and receive video replies. By using videos to support peer-discussion, instructors leverage the power of asynchronous video to build community. Asynchronous video allows learners to put names to faces and creates a deeper level of personalization for online students. Videos can be fun, lighthearted, and creative. The authenticity and self-disclosure video offers can help contribute to students' sense of community. Instructors are increasingly incorporating video discussion threads into their courses. Lowenthal et al. (2020) wrote about how they used such tools in the early days of the COVID-19 pandemic. They found that the use of asynchronous video for discussion allowed for instructors to have more personalized interactions with students, especially those who lived in different time zones. Students were able to asynchronously check in with their colleagues and share mental health resources and stress management techniques. Instructors might consider how the use of video and video threads can help create a more personalized learning experience for students. Video, asynchronously or synchronously, creates a level of intimacy for students that is critical to maintaining a sense of community.

Video Feedback

Incorporating video feedback into online classes is one asynchronous way that instructors can help cultivate community. In a study exploring the reactions of 126 undergraduate and postgraduate students to instructors' 5-minute videos, Henderson and Phillips (2015) found that students preferred video feedback to text-based feedback. Students found video feedback to be specific, personalized, supportive, caring, and motivating. Additionally, students felt video feedback was clearer, more constructive, and prompted greater reflection on course work than text-based feedback. Research suggests that students associate video with greater levels of detail and care (Atwater et al., 2017). Other researchers have found that students find video feedback less intimidating than written feedback. Students might feel more comfortable with feedback when they can hear an instructors' tone and see their body language. Instructors also might be more likely to provide affirmative feedback when recording their reflections on students' work. All of these positive feelings help students cultivate trust, a foundational element of community.

While video feedback can be a great asset to online instructors, it is not without its limitations. Some students can feel anxiety in reviewing video feedback. Other students may not enjoy the pace of video feedback. Unlike written feedback, skimming video feedback can be harder for some students. Additionally, aligning oral feedback to a written assignment can also be challenging, and students might spend extra time trying to make a connection between what was discussed in a video and what might change in their writing. Creating video feedback can also be time-intensive for faculty. Depending on the course load, course size, or on other demands, faculty might not have the time to create videos responding to each students' work. Instructors might consider using video feedback sparsely and strategically. Another strategy is for the instructor to prepare a single video that summarizes common issues the instructor noticed in the assignment while maintaining written customized feedback for each student.

Asynchronous Tools, Learning, and Community

Because students do not meet simultaneously, much of students' interactions in an asynchronous course are with the instructor. Asynchronous courses require a high degree of self-management and lend themselves to more independent learners. The autodidactic nature of asynchronous courses can be isolating, particularly for students that struggle to proactively engage with faculty or create academic and social support networks. However, the tools used in asynchronous courses can still promote community for online students. Discussion boards allow all participants to contribute, which will heighten students' sense of connection to peers. Depending on the topic and facilitation of a discussion board, these spaces can provide opportunities for reflection and self-disclosure, which can strengthen students' sense of community. Asynchronous video content, particularly if it is created by the instructor, can also heighten students' sense of connection to the course. Instructors in asynchronous courses can create personalized resources that speak to students individually and as a collective as a way to promote community-maintenance.

TABLE 3.2
Strengths of Asynchronous Learning Technologies

Asynchronous Feature	Learning Opportunity
Discussion Boards	• Allow for in-depth conversation and wait time for reflection • Equity—everyone can participate
Asynchronous Video Content	• Students can watch at their own pace • Students can pause, forward, or rewind videos for clarification • Instructors can personalize video to meet the needs of different classes
Asynchronous Video Feedback	• Personal, intimate, supportive, caring, motivating

Synchronous Tools in Online Courses: Inside the Virtual Classroom

In an asynchronous course, the LMS also functions as a virtual classroom. It is the primary space where students interact with the instructor and engage in learning activities. In a synchronous course, Web conferencing software is typically the foundation of the virtual classroom. Web conferencing software allows participants to use the internet to join a shared meeting. While the features of Web conferencing software vary by provider, they typically involve video conferencing and some form of chat or direct message.

Some Web conferencing software include additional collaboration feature ssuch as application sharing, polling, interactive whiteboards, emoticons, and breakout rooms. Examples of Web conferencing software that are commonly used as virtual classrooms include Adobe Connect, Blackboard collaborate, WebEx, and Saba Centra. More recently, Zoom has been used as a virtual classroom.

Virtual classrooms can support learning in numerous ways. The real time interaction that the virtual classroom affords has been associated with increased student engagement. Students and instructors can have ongoing discussions, without the lag time of asynchronous communication (Gedera, 2014). Additionally, students and instructors the synchronous virtual classroom can mirror the face-to-face classroom. The opportunities for instant large and small group collaboration can mimic the in-person experience in ways that students find valuable.

The virtual classroom can also provide learning experiences that are harder to re-create in person. For example, some students and technologists have remarked that in a virtual classroom there is "no back row," as all students are in the same sight line. Berry (2017b) felt that the increased visibility of a virtual classroom led to increased student engagement. Additionally, virtual classrooms allow for collaborative tools that might be more efficient than the tools in an in-person class. For example, digital whiteboards allow students to engage in collaborative writing. Unlike on a physical whiteboard, students using a digital whiteboard can easily save their collaborative work.

However, many factors can impair student engagement in virtual classrooms. To successfully participate, students need reliable internet access and a device that supports the Web conference. This increasingly means a computer, tablet, or laptop with a working camera and microphone. Some students, including those who live in rural communities, urban communities experiencing digital redlining, and students who are otherwise socioeconomically disadvantaged, might find it difficult to access internet speeds that are high enough to participate effectively in synchronous sessions. To address this, institutions should make clear the minimum technical requirements for synchronous course participation and provide support to students who are having difficulty meeting these requirements.

An effective synchronous instructor will

- skillfully use multiple features of the Web conferencing system (e.g., breakout rooms, chat);
- integrate student activity through audio, video, and chat; and
- incorporate all students into discussions and activities.

Learning and Community-Building Opportunities Provided by Video Conferencing

As telecommunication systems improve and internet speeds increase, the use of video in virtual classrooms has become increasingly popular. While many researchers have not considered the benefits of video to online learning, a small body of research suggests that it can be highly impactful. One asset of video is that it helps to simulate the face-to-face environment (Knapp, 2018; Martin & Parker, 2014). Students can see the body language of their instructors and peers, which increases teaching presence and help students feel more comfortable with their peers and with their instructor (Rudd & Rudd, 2014; VanOostveen et al., 2018). Students can also get an immediate response from an instructor and from peers, something that has also been associated with enhancing engagement.

A study by Berry (2019b) found that the use of video greatly impacted online students' sense of community. Unlike in a face-to-face classroom, participants in a virtual classroom can see each other equally. The increased visibility videoconferencing affords can incentivize participation, which heightens engagement. Additionally, Berry (2019b) found that the use of video in online courses created greater intimacy between students. Because students were often participating in online classes from their homes, peers were able to get a glimpse into the personal lives of their colleagues. Students would see personal items and family members and used this to make connections to each other. Being in each other's homes or curated spaces can strengthen feelings of connectedness. In all of these ways, synchronous video can heighten online students' sense of community. At the same time, some students will be uncomfortable with the use of video for these same reasons. Some video conferencing software allow for the use of virtual backgrounds, which can give users a greater sense of privacy.

Managing Zoom Fatigue

Zoom fatigue, or cognitive fatigue, refers to the cognitive and physical exhaustion that can occur with prolonged video conferencing use. There are several strategies instructors can use to reduce Zoom fatigue, including

- incorporating frequent breaks into classes
- encouraging students to step away from screens periodically, particularly during breaks
- considering video-optional time periods in long class sessions
- reminding students to limit multitasking, as doing multiple tasks simultaneously increases fatigue
- showing students how to remove desktop distractions like screen view

Learning Opportunities Provided by the Chat Feature

Chat rooms are another important feature of virtual classrooms. Some software have chat rooms embedded in them, so that participants can see each other, and also chat to each other. Some software also have a direct messaging function, where participants can send private messages to peers and/or instructors.

There are many ways to use the chat functions in an online class. Instructors might use the chat as an informal space where students can share reactions and reflections, or more formally as a space to facilitate whole group dialogue. Instructors might also allow the chat to be a space for parallel discussion, where students are talking about something that is related to the course but is not the main discussion. The chat in a virtual classroom can also be a space for light, social conversation. Some chats also allow for direct messaging, allowing users greater privacy.

There are many benefits to allowing a text-based chat to occur in a virtual classroom. Some students perceive chat rooms to be a space where all students have equal access to participating in a course (Berry, 2019b). Unlike oral communication, all students can engage in text-based communication simultaneously. The chat allows for all participants to share, and this shared information can also generate new knowledge for students (McDaniels & Barnacle, 2016). Berry (2019b) found that online students used the chat space to broaden the main discussion through parallel conversations related to course content. Students could also use the chat to shift group discussions by posing questions, affirming comments, or contesting what was being discussed. The embedded chat also helped the instructor and students quickly identify students' questions, and address key concerns in class, rather than waiting until later.

Students who are shyer or who are disinclined to speak out loud will appreciate the easy access of the chat. Chats are also beneficial because they allow participants to intentionally replicate some of the nonverbal components of a face-to-face class. Students can use emoticons to react and express support (applause), dislike (thumbs down), agreement or comprehension (thumbs up). Some platforms are adding more emoticons, including signals for questions and breaks.

Online instructors have the opportunity to use the chat in ways that meet the needs of their particular classrooms. Two important decisions surrounding online chat are determining how and when it should be used.

Figure 3.1. Strategies for maximizing the online chat space.

- Create norms around when and how chat should be used.
- Establish designated breaks in the course session to review chat comments and respond to them.
- Be mindful of accessibility issues regarding chat. Students using assistive technologies may have difficulty managing a chat room and an oral discussion simultaneously. Reach out to students with different learning needs and respond accordingly.
- If chats are particularly robust, consider providing a transcript after class so that students can review it.

Determine How the Chat Should Be Used

- Is it beneficial for the chat to be an open space for ongoing discussion, or should it be used only for questions directed to the instructor?
- Can students use the chat to have parallel discussions that are related to course topics? Can students use the chat to engage in social conversations?

Determine When the Chat Should Be Used

- Some Web conferencing software allow for instructors to disable the chat. Instructors might create times in the course where the chat is open and times when the chat is closed, to better organize the flow of information.
- Instructors might also leave the chat open, but only answer it periodically, during structured times. Instructors should be clear about how frequently they will be responding to chat. Instructors might also encourage students to use other functions, like hand-raising, to bring attention to urgent, time-sensitive questions.
- Instructors might encourage students to reserve the chat for simple questions and comments and ask students to ask more complex questions aloud.

Polls and the Synchronous Classroom

Polls allow instructors to quickly survey their classes. Like clickers in face-to-face classrooms, virtual polls allow each student to participate to express themselves. Polling can be beneficial in groups of any size, but is particularly helpful in large groups, where having each student share out loud can be time-consuming. Polls can be set to anonymous, which might increase students' comfort in sharing about certain topics. Or, polls can allow instructors and the group to see respondents, which can spark student engagement.

Polls can add variety to an online class and increase classroom participation. Instructors might ask more social and interest-oriented questions to get to know students. Or, instructors might use polls as a form of assessment, quizzing students about content knowledge. The real-time data provided by polls can help instructors quickly assess prerequisite knowledge, and instructors can use this data to shape lectures and course discussions. Polls can also be used as a postactivity assessment. For example, after students participate in a breakout room, an instructor might use a poll to assess comprehension. Polling can also be used to quickly check for understanding and establish consensus, which is beneficial in online settings, where mood and body language are more difficult to interpret.

Using Synchronous Tools Together to Promote Community

Video conferences offer users distinct advantages in cultivating community. The ability to see and hear each other in real time provides participants with instant engagement. By allowing everyone to participate simultaneously, chat rooms create another space for increased engagement. Students might express humor or ask probing questions in the chat, which can help strengthen the learning community. Breakout rooms allow instructors to develop smaller, collaborative groups of students. These small groups provide increased opportunities for peer interaction and provide a space for deeper, more meaningful connection. Polls allow for users to privately share feedback with the collective, promoting authentic sharing. Virtual whiteboards can enhance students' feelings of collaboration and interactivity.

While the tools independently provide unique opportunities for interaction, it is the dynamic interplay between them that also enhances students' sense of community. As a result, instructors should be mindful of how to integrate the tools together seamlessly to maximize their affordances. Failing to do so might have an adverse impact on students' experiences. For example, students can become distracted, confused, or disengaged when instructors that allow chat in the online class but do not monitor chats or integrate them into class discussions. Students can also experience confusion in unstructured breakout room activities. An instructors' skillful use of the tools in a virtual classroom can help students engage in a variety of interactions and positively impact their participation in the larger group. Toward that end, online instructors should only use tools they can manage, and continue to build skills to be able to seamlessly integrate new tools into the online class.

The aforementioned strategies provide a starting point for leveraging technology to create community. However, online instructors would be remiss to not acknowledge the ways in which common uses of technology can create unique contextual challenges for historically marginalized students. To cultivate strong online learning communities, instructors must consider the needs of all students, including those with disabilities, remote, rural, low-income, and BIPOC students as well as those who are nonnative speakers of English.

Technology and Disability in the Online Class: The POUR Framework

Online courses should be accessible for all people, including people with online disabilities. One important way to support greater accessibility is

TABLE 3.3
Summary of Learning and Community-Building Opportunities Provided by Synchronous Tools

Synchronous Feature	Learning and Community-Building Opportunities
Videoconferencing	• Supports feelings of connection and closeness (intimacy) • Allows for immediate reactions (immediacy)
Chat	• Supports a range of conversations • Allows everyone to participate simultaneously • Enables students to communicate privately with instructor and/or peers
Breakout Rooms	• Create a space for collaborative work
Polls	• Allow everyone to participate simultaneously • Enable a quick assessment of knowledge and opinions • Support consensus building
Virtual Whiteboards	• Support collaboration and collective brainstorming • Allow users to mark up a shared document • Support file sharing, which can help with collaboration

to ensure that Web content is accessible to all users. The Web Accessibility Initiative (WAI) develops international guidelines for Web accessibility, and the National Center on Accessible Educational Materials (AEM) has further distilled these guidelines into the POUR framework. According to this framework, an accessible user experience is one that is perceivable, operable, understandable, and robust.

According to the National Center on Accessible Educational Materials (AEM), "Perceivable content is presented in a way that it can be accessed with more than one sense" (National Center on Accessible Educational Materials, 2021, para. 1). For example, content that can be accessed visually and auditorily would have greater perceivability than content that can only be accessed by viewing or hearing. Adding alternative text, closed captioning on videos, and providing transcripts are all strategies to increase perceivability, especially for those who are deaf and hard of hearing. In designing course Web pages and learning materials, educators should also use other strategies to increase perceivability, including making sure text is readable and legible to support students with low vision or other learning and cognitive disabilities. To help with visual processing, educators should increase the contrast between text and background and make sure that content doesn't rely solely on color.

Operable content can be easily navigated by all learners. To increase operability, Web content should have a clear organizational structure with headings, labels, and descriptors that make the Web page easier to navigate. AEM notes that links should be descriptive to support use for all students, particularly those who are blind or visually impaired. Educators should avoid links that are vague, such as "click here" or "learn more," and add as much description as is possible, so that students can more easily navigate course pages.

AEM encourages educators to make sure that courses are as understandable as possible. Understandability includes how users are to navigate the course website, and also how they are to make sense of the learning activities therein. Using clear, simple language to explain course expectations and assignments is an important step in increasing accessibility. For students with cognitive disabilities, clear, plain language will help with information processing. Other strategies to increase understandability include detailed directions, models of exemplary work and rubrics to guide participation and assignment completion. As with many elements of accessibility, increasing understandability supports all learners, not just those with disabilities. English language learners will also benefit from efforts to make courses as understandable as possible.

Finally, Web content should be robust, meaning that it is accessible via a variety of current and even future platforms. One way educators can ensure that their content is robust is to test it on a variety of platforms. How does a course page or assignment description appear on a tablet or mobile device? This is an area where instructors might solicit the feedback of their students to help support their own understanding. By ensuring that a course is accessible across platforms, educators give persons with disabilities greater flexibility over when and how they learn. Additionally, students who face challenges to online learning, including low-income students who might lack access to computers or rely on mobile phones for online learning will benefit greatly from courses that work on a wide range of devices.

Utilizing Technology to Support Remote, Rural, and Low-Income Students: Considerations for Equity

While there are many benefits to online learning, every student may not have access to these benefits. Remote, rural, and low-income students may experience difficulties accessing he internet, which can adversely impact their participation in online courses and programs. In developing online learning opportunities, educators and administrators should reflect on who their programs are designed to serve, and how the technologies employed in the academic program meet the needs of those students.

A key consideration for determining instructional delivery and format should be bandwidth. Bandwidth is the amount of data that can be transmitted via the internet per a given unit of time. It is closely related to internet speed. Typically, the greater the internet bandwidth a network has, the faster the internet speed. Two factors impacting internet bandwidth are cost and location. Typically, higher-speed internet costs more than lower-speed internet. This presents an obvious challenge for low-income students. Additionally, not all locations have equal access to high-speed internet. Rural communities are much less likely to have access to high-speed internet than their urban counterparts (Turner, 2016). Fewer service providers offering fewer choices, less telecommunication infrastructure, and inefficient and highly variable wireless options make accessing the internet difficult in rural areas (Holmes & Zubak-Skees, 2015). Many individuals in remote locations rely on mobile phones for internet connection, but coverage is highly variable based on location. American Indians and others who live on tribal lands may also struggle with internet access (U.S. Government Accountability Office, 2016). According to the FCC (2020) only 68% of people living on tribal lands have access to high-speed internet. There are many reasons for these disparities, including high poverty rates, rugged terrain that makes high-quality internet infrastructure difficult, and utility company's underinvestment in internet expansion to rural and tribal communities (U.S. Government Accountability Office, 2016).

Disparities in internet access have implications for teaching and learning. Without sufficient bandwidth, students will have difficulty downloading files, navigating LMSs or course websites, using the internet for course-related research, and streaming audio and video for synchronous virtual classes. Students who are barred from high-speed internet due to cost or location might miss out on learning, especially in classes that require high-bandwidth tasks. Additionally, students with bandwidth issues miss out on opportunities to participate in the classroom community. If technology-related challenges make classroom participation difficult, students will miss out on opportunities to interact with peers and may struggle in developing feelings of membership, belonging, and trust.

Stanford (2020) encourages educators to consider a mix of higher- and lower-bandwidth tasks (discussion boards, reading, email, collaborative documents, and group chat). He developed a bandwidth immediacy matrix to highlight the range of tasks that can occur in an online class and where they relate to bandwidth.

Figure 3.2. Bandwidth immediacy matrix.

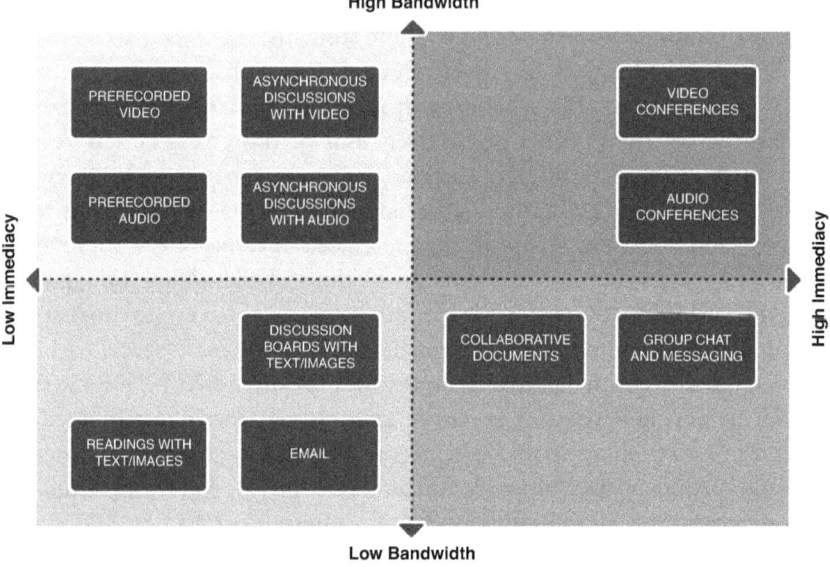

It should be noted that there is a tradeoff between lower bandwidth and a sense of immediacy. In a practical sense, immediacy refers to how quickly individuals can respond to each other. In a synchronous space, participants can respond much more quickly than they can asynchronously. Immediacy also refers to the feeling of intimacy that is produced through a quick, personalized response. Students might feel less immediacy in a course that relies primarily on low-bandwidth tasks like reading and discussion boards than they would in a course that utilizes more synchronous communication. In the bottom right of the matrix, Stanford (2020) provides examples of tasks that provide "practical immediacy" and can support a quick response while using less bandwidth than a video conference. These include the use of collaborative documents and group messaging. These activities can help reduce bandwidth-related challenges while providing online students with ways to connect to the learning community. While these are viable alternatives to higher-bandwidth tasks, students without access to mobile devices or with limited mobile data plans can still experience challenges with these choices. Educators should survey their students and design around their needs.

Addressing Zoom Bombings and Harrassment in Online Classrooms

As the COVID-19 epidemic of 2020 forced many institutions to rapidly adapt, many turned to Web conferencing software like Zoom to facilitate meetings and deliver online instruction. Many institutions were hit with "Zoom bombings," which are racist, misogynistic, and pornographic intrusions shared with groups by unwelcome participants (Redden, 2020). Such attacks can undermine underrepresented students' sense of community in the online classroom. These intrusions undermine students' feelings of trust and safety in the learning environment, and the content shared can undermine students' sense of membership and belonging in the learning community. As educators seek out a range of platforms to deliver synchronous instruction, they must be aware of how their courses and students may be targeted for racist and sexist harassment. Administrators and support staff should also provide instructors with information about how to keep online synchronous courses as safe as possible. (See Figure 3.3 for a summary of safety strategies for online courses.)

Considerations for Administrators

The information explored in this chapter provides many considerations for administrators, particularly as it relates to program development and management. One of the first factors an administrator must consider in establishing an online program is whether or not courses will be offered synchronously, asynchronously, or via a hybrid model. As the chapter highlights, each format provides opportunities and limitations for communication and connection. Administrators should align the program structure with the needs of students. This means thinking about how a student population might benefit

Figure 3.3. Strategies for keeping online courses safe from "Zoom bombings" and unwanted intrusion.

- Require passwords for meetings.
- Enable a waiting room to monitor the entrance of participants into a Web conference.
- Limit participants' ability to screen share.
- Mute participants upon entry.
- Disable private chats.

or struggle in different online course formats. For example, students who had academic challenges prior to enrollment might struggle with the independent nature of asynchronous courses. Working professionals, individuals with busy personal schedules, and students with strong time-management skills might enjoy the asynchronous format. Students who are returning to higher education after long gaps and/or students who are new to online learning may benefit from the support offered by synchronous or blended courses.

Administrators should design online programs around the unique needs of their context. This also means embedding necessary supports to help mitigate the challenges and maximize opportunities provided by different online course formats. For example, program directors might consider how to facilitate synchronous student interactions in the online program, to capitalize on the affordance of intimacy synchronicity provides. Administrators should also consider the role of asynchronous and synchronous support in reaching out to online students who are struggling or desire extra support. Leaders in online programs might also consider how they orient students to online programs, so that students are aware of and prepared to meet any challenges that arise.

In considering the impact of different technologies on the learning experience, this chapter also provides administrators with an opportunity to consider what full and equitable participation in an online course looks like. This in turn allows administrators to think about any specific challenges students face in different online formats. For example, synchronous courses, for all of their benefits, are challenging for students without access to high-speed internet. Given that disparities in internet access disproportionately impact students of color, low-income students, and individuals in rural or tribal communities, this becomes an equity issue. Administrators should encourage faculty to diversify the learning activities in online classes, so that students with variable access to technology still can access instruction. Stanford's (2020) bandwidth and immediacy matrix provides a mix of high- and low-bandwidth activities that can be beneficial for under resourced students.

The concept of affordances as a whole can also be useful in helping instructors think about what different technologies actually do. Online learning is not simply about format—synchronous, asynchronous, or hybrid. The quality of an online course is impacted by how instructors maximize the potential of the tools at their disposal. When administrators understand the various learning opportunities and affordances that different types of technologies can support, they are better positioned to know which aspects of faculty development are important for their academic programs.

This chapter also provided key considerations for supporting diverse learners in online environments. A core component of inclusion is accessibility. Ensuring that students with varying abilities and disabilities can participate in online classrooms is a key component of fostering a sense of community for all students. Institutions can help build faculty capacity in this area by investing in quality assurance programs, and/or by encouraging greater collaboration between instructors, faculty developers, and instructional designers.

Safety is another core component of inclusion and is a vital prerequisite for community. Online administrators should note that technology creates opportunities for increased visibility, and with it, provides opportunities for greater surveillance and intrusion. For example, the use of video in synchronous online courses provides students and instructors with the opportunity to have intimate awareness of others' personal spaces. This can lead to increased scrutiny of some students, including scrutiny with racist, sexist, or classist undertones. Virtual backgrounds and cultural sensitivity training can help reduce some of these microaggressions. On a more macrolevel, administrators must ensure that all faculty know how to keep their online courses safe from unwanted intrusion. Zoom bombings often take racist and sexist overtones, and therefore place BIPOC students, women, and sexual minority students at greater risk. Administrators should collaborate with technical support and other divisions to ensure that maximum security is used in online courses.

Considerations for Instructional Designers, Faculty Developers, and Other Staff in Centers for Teaching and Learning

Instructional designers, faculty developers, and staff in centers for teaching and learning are well-positioned to help faculty make informed decisions about how to structure online courses in an effective, engaging, and community-oriented way. For example, instructional designers can give faculty insight about how to overcome the isolation that can occur in asynchronous courses by encouraging the use of discussion boards and asynchronous video content and feedback. They can help faculty learn how to leverage the affordances of synchronous technologies and provide hands-on sessions where faculty practice using tools in a virtual classroom; including breakout rooms, polls, and chat. Faculty developers can also encourage greater awareness, sensitivity, and planning around students lived experiences of learning with technology, including how to support students with short-term or long-term internet challenges.

Instructional designers and faculty developers will play a key role in helping faculty leverage the potential of institutionally offered technology, including virtual classrooms and LMSs. These staff will also play a key role in making sure that faculty use these and other tools in ways that are accessible to all students. Because support staff cannot measure each class or every learning activity, they should be mindful of how they build faculty capacity in the area of accessibility. Trainings and support programs that focus specifically on the accessible use of technology are essential, and administrators should provide resources specifically for this aspect of faculty development.

Conclusion

Technology plays a central role in online students' experiences. The temporal aspects of a course influence not only when, but how students connect. The features of the virtual classroom, particularly discussion boards, video, and chat, provide different opportunities for learning and peer interaction. Educators and administrators should consider the affordances and limitations of various online formats, tools, and technologies when developing an online course or program. The next two chapters delve deeper into the teaching strategies and practices online instructors can do to maximize the opportunities provided by asynchronous and synchronous learning, using these formats to create dynamic learning communities.

4

ASYNCHRONOUS TEACHING PRACTICES THAT SUPPORT ONLINE COMMUNITY

An asynchronous course can feel distant and mysterious to students. Instructors can combat these feelings by striking a warm and welcoming tone before the course begins. As mentioned in chapter 2 (this volume), a welcome letter is a beneficial tool that can help the students learn about the instructor and their expectations for the course. Riggs and Linder (2016) recommend providing a full course orientation to the asynchronous course, where the instructor can provide a detailed overview of the course structure, expectations, and requirements. This orientation might include a tour of the LMS, as this is where the bulk of asynchronous interactions will occur. Riggs and Linder also suggest the use of video or voice-over screen tools so that instructors can show students how to use the LMS. In the video tour, instructors can show students how to access the syllabus and how to utilize the other tools for course communication and collaboration. Video or voice-over screen can be more engaging and easier to follow for a detailed overview than a letter.

Setting the tone for community, especially in an asynchronous course, requires allowing students to share about themselves as well. As noted in chapter 2 (this volume), instructors can do this in asynchronous courses by creating a discussion board where students are invited to share personal information like location, interests, hobbies, and professional information; as well as career aspirations. Students can also share multimedia as they are comfortable, including short videos or photographs. Instructors might use apps like Flipgrid to engage in ongoing video-based discussions. This personalization might strengthen students' sense of community.

As an asynchronous course gets underway, instructors might think about the types of guides and supports that will be used to facilitate learning. While a key feature of asynchronous courses is the ability to navigate asynchronous content independently, many students will need support in doing this, especially in the early stages of the online course. To help students build their skills, instructors can create scaffolding materials that help students understand how they should be processing information in the course. Graphic organizers can be a useful tool in supporting comprehension. Instructors can also create printable and downloadable listening, viewing, and reading guides, so that students have guided questions they can answer as they engage with course material (Johnson, 2021).

After the initial tone and format of the class are established, instructors can employ various learning activities and pedagogical strategies to strengthen community asynchronously. It is to this topic that we turn our attention.

Asynchronous Learning Activities

One of the most common ways to design an asynchronous course is to focus directly on student–instructor interactions. While submitting assignments to instructors and receiving individual feedback is helpful for learning, it does not provide students with many opportunities for peer interaction, and does not help strengthen students' sense of community. Asynchronous instructors can use a range of learning activities to support interaction, collaboration, and community. These activities include:

- digital social reading and annotation to help students learn content, and quizzes and tests to assess learning
- discussion boards to help students evaluate course content and develop shared meaning of information
- creative assignments like blogs, wikis, podcasts, and portfolios that can promote reflection and stimulate cognitive presence

Using a variety of assignment types in an asynchronous course creates a wide range of options for increasing collaboration and supporting community.

Digital Social Reading and Annotation

With digital social reading, students and instructors can read and annotate a shared text. Students can make comments and questions in digital files, and instructors can respond to student comments. Instructors might also proactively annotate a text with video, audio, or written comments, to help guide students' understanding of content. In a meta-analysis of articles on the topic, Zhu et al. (2020) found that Web annotation had at least five benefits—it helped students process domain specific knowledge, supported argumentation and inquiry, improved students' literacy skills, supported instructor and peer assessment, and helped students connect in online spaces. Additionally, the social and collaborative nature of digital social reading and annotation make it an effective strategy for building community.

Quizzes and Tests

Instructors can embed assessment into their content. Whether using an annotated or interactive text or using a module in a LMS, integrating reflection and comprehension questions into course readings or videos is one way to check for students' understanding of course content. Some systems require successful completion of the assessment before the student is able to complete the reading or module. Embedded assessments allow both the student and the instructor to monitor comprehension and progress, and can strengthen student engagement by making learning more active.

Blogs and Wikis in Asynchronous Courses

Whereas a journal is typically a private or semiprivate writing space, a blog is a more public way of publishing reflective writing on the internet. Blogs can be beneficial for engaging in both personal and public reflection. Blogs are often topical or thematic, and can be an individual process, or a blog can have multiple contributors. Wikis allow students to collaboratively write and edit content online. While wikis can include personal reflections, they are typically more formal and content-oriented than blogs. Students can use wikis to analyze and organize course material, to share presentations, and to create shared resources, including a creative or informational project. Wikis can be public or semiprivate (restricted only to the group). Wikis allow content to be buildable over time, and can be used between classes and cohorts as an evolving repository for information on a particular topic.

Blogs and wikis are important for cultivating community. Blogging promotes self-disclosure, which in turn can promote a deeper sense of authenticity and intimacy in the learning environment. Wikis can allow for peer collaboration, which is also an important community builder. As students negotiate their shared work, they are more likely to develop deeper bonds between each other.

Podcasts in Asynchronous Courses

Podcasts are another way to build connections between students and their peers, and between students and the academic content. An instructor can assign a podcast that is created by someone else as a way to illustrate or elaborate on core course content. Podcasts can also be used to provide social and historical context, explain important issues, and provide diverse perspectives to students. By listening to podcasts, students can be exposed to a range of different perspectives, and can learn different ways to talk about a particular subject. Instructors can also create their own podcasts for students, and use the audio files as a way to explain course content. This adds greater personalization to a course, something that online students will find beneficial.

Some instructors have taken podcast use a step further by asking students to create their own. Students can learn many skills from the podcast process, including research, interviewing, and public speaking. Podcasts also allow students to share what they have learned not only with their peers, but with the broader community. Students may find this to be a particular asset of podcasting, as they can share academic content to the broader world in a relatable way.

Portfolios in Asynchronous Courses

Portfolios can be cumulative, or can be compiled at a designated point in the course. Instructors might have students reflect before or after a particular unit or activity, or at the end of a unit or course. Reflections can also center on different aspects of the course, such as participation, group work, or on the development of a particular skill (Johnson, 2021). Portfolios can also be helpful at the program level, as students and instructors can monitor students' progress toward the development of particular skills or competencies over time and across curriculum. The deep reflection afforded by portfolios helps cultivate cognitive presence and enriches students' connection to academic content. This, in turn, supports students' sense of community. Portfolios also have utility outside of the class. Students can use them to highlight achievements and display field-based and applied projects, something that might be of interest to prospective employers.

Collaboration and Community-Building in Asynchronous Courses

Some students are drawn to asynchronous classes because they provide flexibility and independence. Instructors can maintain these vital elements while also providing opportunities for collaboration and peer interaction.

TABLE 4.1
Asynchronous Activities That Build Community

Asynchronous Activity	Community-Building Connection
Digital Social Reading and Annotation	Students can see their peers' meaning-making processes, and work together to create a shared understanding.
Blogs and Wikis	These websites support more prolonged engagement around course content, and provide opportunities for students to learn about different facets of their peers. Additionally, these types of projects can encourage perspective taking, something that can strengthen empathy and enhance feelings of belonging.
Podcasts	These audio broadcasts support more prolonged engagement around course content, and provide opportunities for students to learn about different facets of their peers. Additionally, these types of projects can encourage perspective taking, something that can strengthen empathy and enhance feelings of belonging. The connections provided by multimedia production can strengthen cognitive presence, a deeper form of learning that strengthens' students' engagement to the content and to the course.
Portfolios	By allowing students to showcase learning and accomplishments, portfolios provide a space for peers to provide affirmation for their colleagues' accomplishments.

The aforementioned asynchronous activities allow for varied levels of peer-to-peer engagement and can strengthen online students' sense of community. Table 4.1 highlights asynchronous tools and activities that build community.

Discussion Boards: A Key Component of Asynchronous Courses

Because discussion boards are a mainstay in online classes, particularly asynchronous ones, a significant portion of this chapter focuses on how to facilitate boards that are engaging and interactive. In this section, I explore the different types of discussion boards, their uses and benefits, and strategies for increasing participation and collaboration.

Discussion Boards: Uses and Benefits

Discussion boards offer several unique benefits to students. One benefit of discussion boards is that they allow students to respond to prompts and to peers at their own pace. The added time can lend to stronger writing and deeper reflection. Additionally, unlike synchronous discussions, asynchronous discussion boards allow students to respond to as many people as they want, with as much detail as they like. The time for added reflection and in-depth processing can help students develop writing skills.

Additionally, because discussion boards are often shorter than academic papers, they provide students with an opportunity to practice being concise, a skill that is helpful for professional writing (Foushee, 2018). Another asset of discussion boards is that they allow students to learn more about how their peers approach assignments. By reviewing their colleagues' work, students can strengthen their own writing skills. Students also report higher self-efficacy when they are able to compare their work to their peers via a discussion board (Harrington & Aloni, 2018). The ability to share with peers can help students cultivate feelings of connection in online classrooms. Discussion boards can also become highly interactive, supporting a wide range of conversations and collaborative learning activities. In this way, discussion boards become a tool for facilitating online community (Berry, 2019b). This can even be true in synchronous or hybrid courses. Discussion boards can be a valuable connection point for students and instructors in between synchronous sessions. As such, they are a vital tool for community maintenance.

Different Types of Discussion Boards

Traditional academic discussion boards allow students to respond to curriculum-related prompts. These boards are usually graded, and responses can be reflective or fact-based. However, using discussion boards to respond to academic content is only one way to use them. Table 4.2 highlights other uses of discussion boards in asynchronous courses.

Discussion Boards and Community

Discussion boards can be a powerful tool for community development and maintenance, if instructors are intentional about creating them in this way. For example, prior to, or at the start of the academic term, discussion boards can be used as a space for "getting to know you" activities and icebreakers. Students can share via text, audio, or video. This type of sharing can be especially beneficial for asynchronous students, as they might lack other formal

TABLE 4.2
Types and Purposes of Discussion Boards

Type of Discussion Board	Purpose of Discussion Board
Introductions and Ice-Breakers	These activities provide a space for virtual introductions and other "getting to know you" activities. Students can share text, audio, or video introductions.
Socialization and Peer Interaction	These relations establish a designated space for ongoing dialogue about topics of personal interest. Boards can be general or separated by topic.
Question and Answer Forums and Parking Lots	This workflow process creates a space for questions that have yet to be answered, including questions that should be addressed later in the course (parking lot).
Pre-assessment and Post-assessment	Students can share written reflections that highlight their understanding of course content. Students can share before or after a reading, learning activity, or module.

opportunities for getting to know their peers. For synchronous students, using the boards in this way can allow a space for students to start making connections and building rapport, while saving synchronous meetings for more in-depth work.

During the term, discussion boards can be a vital space for peer-to-peer interaction. If a class is based solely on interactions between the instructor and the individual student, a student may feel disconnected from the larger classroom community. By creating experiences for peer interaction, instructors are also supporting student engagement, and, in turn, retention. Instructors can require students to respond to one or many of their peers' posts, in an effort to spark dialogue. Instructors can also use discussion boards for more collaborative activities, including role play and debate. Varying the types of interactions on discussion boards allows students to connect with different peers in different ways.

Different discussion board topics can also impact students' sense of community. When students are asked to analyze and respectfully challenge their perspectives and their peers' perspectives, they can collaborate and create shared understanding. This type of analysis can increase cognitive presence, which can increase feelings of community.

Understanding What Drives Student Participation in Online Discussion Boards

While discussion boards are important tools for supporting learning, the benefits of discussion boards will not be realized if students do not engage with them. There are many reasons why student participation in online discussion boards may be limited. Some students might not see the need for a particular discussion. This can happen when a learning objective is not clearly outlined. If an instructor does not explain how the discussion board will support understanding of course content, some students will disconnect from the activity (Balaji & Chakrabarti, 2010). Engagement may also be limited when discussion board questions or topics are redundant, referring to topics that have already been discussed in previous assignments. Grading practices also factor into discussion board participation. Some students will be less likely to participate in boards that do not significantly impact their overall grade for the course (Pena-Shaff & Altman, 2015). Instructors can support discussion-board engagement by making clear connections between the prompts, the course topic, other assignments, and grades in the course. Instructors should also explain how participation in specific discussion boards will strengthen students' understanding of course content.

The behavior of other participants also impacts how students engage with discussion boards. If peer responses are vague and superficial, students will become disinterested in the learning activity. This can also happen if peer responses are delayed—or nonexistent. It is important for instructors to create clear guidelines and norms for when and how to participate and respond to discussion boards. Students may be more likely to respond to their peers when they receive credit for these responses. Students can also become inactive if their peers demonstrate too much emotion or a hostile tone in discussion boards. Instructors can manage this proactively by establishing norms for appropriate discourse in a discussion board.

Technology also impacts' discussion board participation. While instructors do not have a lot of flexibility in terms of the LMS their institution uses, it is important to be aware of how technology impacts participation. Different LMSs make different choices regarding the structure of posts, whether participants can create new threads, or whether participants can see the posts by others only after submitting their own post. Instructors should utilize features like "student view" to see what their boards look like from the students' end. Instructors should provide tips for managing their boards with the student view in mind.

Establish Expectations for Successful Participation and Peer Response

Expectations for discussion boards can vary from course-to-course and instructor-to-instructor. It is important for each instructor to communicate clear expectations for what high quality discussion board participation looks like in their course (Dennen, 2005; Pena-Shaff & Altman, 2015). In addressing their basic expectations for a discussion board, instructors should outline

- how long the post should be
- when the post should be submitted
- if the post should include references to other materials, either from the course or from other sources
- if and how references should be cited

Ideally, a discussion board is not used simply for students to respond to questions, but to foster a robust dialogue. To support interactivity, instructors should pose clear initial questions. Including probes and follow-up questions can also promote dialogue and student engagement. Instructors who take an active role in the boards by asking follow-up questions to students might find that their boards are more interactive. However, some students will be lax to respond to instructor follow-ups if they are not sure about how their responses will be assessed. A study by Pena-Shaff and Altman (2015) found that students were more likely to respond to follow-up questions when they knew that they would be graded for their initial and subsequent responses. This finding highlights the importance of clear expectations for all participation in discussion boards, not just the initial post.

Develop Expectations for Peer-to-Peer Responses

Providing substantive responses to peers' posts should be an explicit expectation of discussion threads. Some students will not respond to their peers if they are not required to do so. In some contexts, students view the instructor as the sole expert in the class and may be less interested in learning from their colleagues. It is important to create a classroom culture where students see the value of peer knowledge-sharing, and are incentivized to engage in it.

While requiring peer responses is the first step to creating an interactive discussion board, students need explicit support in how to respond to their peers' online posts. One of the biggest challenges of discussion boards is superficial responses to peers' posts. Students might respond with general niceties (e.g., "amazing post," "I agree with everything in this post") or with vague responses (e.g., "this post is interesting"). There are a variety of reasons for this. Students may be afraid of creating conflict with peers, so they might feel like the best course of action is to create vaguely affirmative responses. Or, students may be unsure of how to extend a discussion. Instructors can preempt some of this confusion by having students analyze and critique mock responses to posts. This can create a safe context for critically examining student responses, and for brainstorming more substantive responses. If the course is already underway, an instructor can attempt to address these patterns by highlighting them, spotlighting stronger student posts (with permission), and asking students to discuss the types of peer responses that are most helpful in their learning.

Align Expectations to Grading Process

Clear grading guidelines are an important component of ensuring active participation in the discussion boards. Aligning expectations of successful board completion to discussion board grades is an easy and clear way to begin to think about how to assess a board. Instructors should also consider the role that the discussion board plays in the overall course grade. Factors to consider include the amount of effort, time on task, and outside research required by the assignment. Instructors should also consider student capacity to complete the boards. Harrington and Thomas (2018) recommend assigning less weight to discussions that take place earlier on in the course, so that students have lower stakes opportunities to respond to feedback.

Rubrics can be useful in grading individual discussion board responses. Rubrics should include all of the work students are expected to do, including peer response. Rubrics can reduce student anxiety and increase successful task completion. See Figure 4.1 for a sample discussion board rubric.

Figure 4.1. Sample discussion board rubric.

A strong discussion post does the following:
- clearly responds to the prompt
- draws on (and cites) the course readings and/or concepts to articulate a position
- is between 300–500 words

A strong response to peers' posts does the following:
- thoughtfully responds to the argument laid out, incorporating course readings and/or core concepts to support the response
- analyzes, critiques, or extends the argument
- is between 100–300 words

Develop Community Agreements for Board Conduct

Successful completion of a discussion board or other online course assignment is not just about finishing the task but doing so in a way that reflects the values of the institution and the course. Toward that end, discussion board conduct is something instructors must consider. If instructors wait until violations have already taken place to address them, they may lose the confidence and trust of some students, undermining students' sense of community. One way to proactively address discussion board conduct is to remind students of the institutions' code of conduct. Instructors might also want to expound upon university expectation and make clear that racist and sexist content will not be tolerated. In an effort to mitigate offensive engagement, instructors should also ask students to refrain from using generalizations or stereotypes. Students should be reminded of the importance of following these rules, as they are important for developing an online course that is inclusive and promotes a safe learning environment for all.

Begin With a Generative Prompt

Participation in boards is influenced significantly by the initial question or prompt (Howell et al., 2017). Open ended questions tend to yield more reflective and detailed responses than close-ended questions. If the answer to the prompt requires a single, fact-based answer, engagement will be limited. Howell et al. (2017) found that divergent questions, questions for which a multiplicity of responses are valid, were more effective than convergent questions, which tend to have a single correct answer. Instructors should consider using discussion prompts that would require a unique response from each participant, rather than prompts that provoke similar answers from respondents. Once a board becomes repetitive, participation will decrease. See Figure 4.2 for information about the relationship between strong discussion board prompts and community.

Bloom's taxonomy provides a useful guide for supporting generative discussion prompts. Questions that require analysis, synthesis and evaluation are more likely to get substantive responses than questions focus solely on memorization and simple comprehension of facts (Jacobi, 2017). Instructors should consider prompts that ask students to

- evaluate information
- defend/critique a position
- generate a wide range of viewpoints on a topic
- share an opinion
- interpret information
- create alternative hypotheses/scenarios

Figure 4.2. Strong discussion board prompts and community.

> Generative prompts create the conditions for deep reflection and peer interaction. Prompts that require students to share their opinions can promote authenticity and self-disclosure. Prompts that encourage students to share viewpoints and personal experiences can promote authenticity. Questions that support a unique response from each student create opportunities for students to share and to learn from all of their peers, which can increase feelings of membership, trust, and belonging.

Instructors should take care to develop discussion prompts that require complex, thoughtful and through responses. However, prompts should not be too difficult, or else it will be hard for students to engage. Prompts should be challenging enough to provoke thought, but simple enough to be understood and completed independently by all students.

Discussion Board Management

Strong prompts create a firm foundation for robust discussion boards. However, boards do not manage themselves. In order to ensure students are actually contributing to and learning from a discussion board, the instructor must take an active role as a manager and facilitator of the board. Strategies for discussion board management are provided in this section.

The Instructor as Discussion Board Moderator

Moderating an online discussion board is a delicate dance that is fundamental to online course management. Instructors must construct questions that are generative enough to produce high-level responses without confusing students or requiring too much additional prompting. Instructors must also take an active role in the boards, without dominating the conversation. Some best practices for moderating discussion boards are to respond to initial student work quickly and within a preestablished time frame. Instructors should also respond quickly to students' follow up questions and comments on the discussion board.

It is important for instructors to reply to as many individual students as possible, so that students know that their posts are being recognized. Replying to students helps reinforce the feeling that they are valued members of an interactive community. Instructors might consider batching responses to students who have similar answers, but should also try to acknowledge each student by name if possible. If the size of the class or the volume of posts make it difficult to respond to each student, the instructor might make clear that each week they will respond to a certain number of posts. Instructors who choose this path should let students know what to expect regarding response time. Other strategies to improve discussion board moderation include helping students establish a rhythm around posting and responding, bringing organization to posts, varying the structure of discussion boards to promote engagement and using comments to extend the discussion.

Helping Students Get Into a Rhythm With Posting and Responding

A discussion board can be a highly engaging space. As such, it is a vital site for community formation. However, connections can only be made when students are actually interacting with peers. Instructors can support peer interaction by structuring participation. Giving due dates for posts and responses helps students manage their interactions with peers, and ensures that students aren't writing (or responding) into a void. Due dates should provide enough time for students to reflect on the posts, but not be so far apart that students forget about the topic. Instructors can also model responsive discussion board behavior by responding swiftly and thoroughly to student posts. Instructors can also prompt peer interaction by asking students who have similar or opposing perspectives to respond to each others' posts.

Bringing Organization to the Posts

While a discussion board can spark a robust conversation, sometimes that conversation diverges from the instructors' initial prompt. Some ways to bring organization to discussion boards include

- encouraging students to label their posts with keywords and phrases so that peers who respond to their posts can more easily identify posts that they might respond to
- managing threaded discussions by creating multiple threads if the discussion becomes too long or unwieldy
- creating multiple boards based on different topics or subtopics, so that discussions become more streamlined

All of these strategies make it easier for students to find relevant information, thereby increasing their participation.

Varying the Structure of Discussion Boards to Promote Engagement

If discussion boards are a regular component in your course, you will want to consider how to vary the structure of the boards so that they are not repetitive. A typical discussion board format is to have students respond to one instructor-generated prompt. This can create a lengthy discussion, and can strengthen cohesion among the class as a whole. However, some students may also grow bored with this format, particularly if it is the only structure used in an asynchronous course. Additionally, some students may feel lost in a large discussion. Research by Akcaoglu and Lee (2016) and others found that students felt more connected to peers and had a more positive overall learning experience when discussion boards were in groups of four to six people rather than in whole group discussion boards. Instructors might try having multiple boards running simultaneously with different questions. Instructors can manage the boards by pre-assigning students to different discussions, or, they can let students choose which boards to participate in. Either way, splitting the boards up by size and topic might allow for respondents to go into greater depth, and will reduce occurrences of repetitive responses.

Another way to add variation to discussion boards is to vary the ways in which the question is posed. Discussion boards usually solicit responses from instructor-generated, text-based questions. Instructors can consider varying the prompt, so that students respond to prompts generated from other sources, including video clips, podcasts, news reports, or research briefs. Student responses do not always have to be text-generated, either. Clark et al. (2015) found that having students respond via video can also be important for increasing social presence. Using video to support discussion can be particularly beneficial in times of crisis. Lowenthal et al. (2020) outlined the various ways they used asynchronous video threads in an asynchronous classroom at the start of the COVID-19 pandemic. The authors used video threads to facilitate group discussions that were centered on student well-being and course updates. One instructor created an ongoing "office hours" video thread where he could respond to questions about course content and create video replies. Instructors might consider how the use of video in an ongoing discussion thread provides both flexibility and interactivity.

Use Comments to Extend the Discussion

Hsieh and Tsai (2012) provided many strategies for supporting asynchronous discussion. They divided their strategies into cognitive strategies, those that would help promote knowledge, and affective strategies, those that would help sustain motivation. The first cognitive strategy was to help students focus on the main topics. They recommended the use of follow up prompts and probing questions to redirect comments that are off topic. The second cognitive strategy was to facilitate the line of argumentation students established. Prompts like, "Why is this message important?" and "Please tell us more about this idea" could be used to extend the discussion and to also focus the attention of other students. Additionally, cognitive prompts could promote deeper and more varied reflection on topics. They also recommended affective strategies such as giving students positive feedback.

Discussion Board Management Strategies and Community

When boards are tightly facilitated, discussion is enriched. Bringing organization and variety to discussion boards ensures that participation is fluid and efficient. With these conditions in place, students can focus on what matters—sharing rich, thought-provoking content that reflects their learning. Instructors who participate actively in discussion boards by asking comments and questions to extend the discussion can provide a model for peer-to-peer interaction as well. Students may attempt to emulate instructors' prosocial discussion board behavior, leading to a more interactive and inclusive learning community.

Discussion Board Teaching Strategy: Peer Facilitation

The previous section focused on the ways in which instructors can moderate online discussion boards. However, instructors might also consider sharing the moderator role with students, and allowing students, either individually or in groups, to serve as peer facilitators of discussion boards. Peer facilitation is when students lead a small group activity (e.g., discussion). As a facilitator or moderator, the student takes on the responsibility of responding to peers, clarifying answers, and giving feedback to their colleagues. In a discussion board, a student moderator would pose a guiding prompt to the group and take the lead on managing the discussion board conversation by responding to peers' comments. Moderators could also summarize important points from the discussion and the course content, ensuring that the discussion is robust, substantive, and easy to follow.

Peer facilitation offers several benefits to students. It allows them to take accountability for their learning in a different way, giving them more agency over the academic task. This can increase engagement and buy-in. Peer facilitation can also promote metacognition among students, as they will be prompted to analyze their own teaching and learning processes. Additionally, peer facilitation helps decenter the role of the instructor. Instead of there being one "sage on stage," peer facilitation positions each member of the classroom as an expert in knowledge construction. As such, peer facilitation is associated with the formation of cognitive presence.

Peer Facilitation and Community

Peer facilitation promotes shared collaboration around learning goals, one of the core components of community. Additionally, the opportunity to engage in collaborative decision making can increase connectedness, and the opportunity to cultivate shared perspectives can lead to enhanced sense of belonging. Student facilitation also gives more students greater opportunity for leadership. In this way, peer facilitation can help promote students' feelings of equity and inclusion in the learning environment.

In a literature review, Chen et al. (2019) identified six types of peer facilitation—questioning, making clarification, promoting connection, summarizing and revoicing, providing information, and using positive social cues. Instructors should model these facilitation techniques and encourage student facilitators to do the same. Students who are acting as moderators can use these strategies to manage a discussion board. Students who are not moderators can use these strategies in their peer responses. Table 4.3 on peer facilitation types has been synthesized from Chen et al.'s (2019) work.

TABLE 4.3
Types of Peer Facilitation

Peer Facilitation Strategies	*The facilitator can:*
Questioning	<ul><li>ask a question that prompts participants to consider "how" and "why"</li><li>ask the learner to explain a position</li><li>ask the learner to provide a fact that supports their assertion</li></ul>
Make Clarifications	<ul><li>encourage participants to explain an idea through elaboration</li><li>ask students to give a "real-world example" to support an assertion</li><li>invite students to develop an analogy to support an argument</li></ul>
Promote Connection	<ul><li>encourage students to draw upon personal experience</li><li>make connections between class content, previous readings, or discussions</li></ul>

(Continued)

TABLE 4.3 (*Continued*)

Peer Facilitation Strategies	The facilitator can:
Summarize and Revoice	• synthesize ideas shared by participants • highlight important and relevant ideas • reflect discussion progress
Provide Information	• provide information from authoritative sources • present alternative perspectives
Use Positive Social Cues	• use compliments to highlight high-quality peer-to-peer interaction • express gratitude for learners' contributions • invite students to participate in the discussion

Teaching Strategy: Role Play on a Discussion Board

Instructors who are looking to take their moderating or peer facilitation activities to the next level might consider role play as a strategy for managing discussions. While the roles adopted might vary based on subject and students' skill level, there are many roles that could be beneficial in an online discussion board. Olesova et al. (2016) assigned students in an online discussion board to the following roles: starter, skeptic, or wrapper. The starter's role was to post an initial response to stimulate discussion, the wrapper summarized key points made in the discussion, and the skeptic's job was to challenge points brought up by students in the discussion. Some instructors assign students to play the role of the "devil's advocate," where they are encouraged to adopt a different perspective and defend it. In an upper level psychology course, Aloni (2016) assigned roles of research reporter, method evaluator, and hypothesis generator. The research reporter found a relevant journal article and summarized it for the class. The method evaluator described the strengths and limitations of the methodology. The hypothesis generator developed follow up hypotheses based on the study. Instructors can modify such an approach to their topic and discipline.

In a role play, instructors should model different strategies of questioning and responding. One inquiry strategy that can be beneficial for student learning, whether they adopt a formal role or simply seek to reflect more deeply on peers' responses, is Socratic questioning. Through Socratic questioning, students ask questions of their peers and course content as a means of arriving at a deeper understanding (Harrington and Aloni, 2013). For example, a student might ask a clarifying question, a question that probes at the respondents' purpose, or a question that asks a respondent to compare and contrast their assertion so as to arrive at a more refined meaning. No matter what approach instructors take, a variety of approaches is important. De Wever et al. (2009) found that students acclimated to discussion board formats over time, and encouraged variety as a way to maintain student engagement. Role play, then, is just one of many tools in the online instructors' toolkit.

Race and Gender Bias in Online Discussions

While researchers have explored expectations and best practices for online discussion boards in general, less attention has been paid to the specific topics of equity and inclusion in online discussion boards. A study by Stanford's Center for Education Policy Analysis in 2018 which looked at the discussion forms of 124 different online courses found that instructors in the study were 94% more likely to respond to forum posts by white male students (Baker et al., 2018). There was not general evidence of biases in student responses, however data suggested that students were more likely to respond to those perceived to be from their own race and gender. Instructors might address this by keeping a log of which students they respond to, to ensure that their responses are equitable. Creating multiple boards and pre-assigning students to them is another way to increase the likelihood that students will respond to a broader, more diverse array of peers.

Discussion boards are not the only spaces where covert and overt discrimination can occur. There are possibilities for microaggressions and macroaggressions in any learning space. Unfortunately, there is a dearth of research on the experiences of BIPOC students in asynchronous environments. Administrators, faculty, and staff should consider how they might collect data on BIPOC students' online experiences and intentionally design learning spaces that meet their needs.

Considerations for Administrators

This chapter reframes asynchronous learning in ways that are important for administrators to consider. While some students are drawn to asynchronous learning because they perceive it to be "independent," this chapter highlights the ways in which collaboration can and should be embedded in asynchronous courses. Interactivity is important to students' engagement and sense of community. Additionally, a more interactive course ensures that there are multiple ways for students to learn course material and demonstrate competency, two factors that are critical in students' academic success. This chapter highlights the high degree of planning, preparation, and coordination needed to create an asynchronous course that is interactive. Administrators must consider how they can prepare, support, and incentivize faculty to implement the broad range of learning activities outlined in this chapter. Additionally, administrators might see the importance of elevating the experiences of faculty who are using strategies and activities like the ones outlined and create opportunities for them to share teaching resources with colleagues and support staff.

While this chapter obviously highlights teaching strategies that can be used in asynchronous courses, it also has implications for work that occurs across courses and throughout academic programs. While asynchronous learning does not have to be totally independent, it does require some autodidactism and self-motivation. At the same time, asynchronous students benefit from clear systems and structures that guide and direct learning. Administrators seeking to create continuity from course to course in an asynchronous or hybrid program might ask themselves the following questions:

- What norms for participation and assignment completion might be transferable from course to course?
- What key assignments or materials can be carried from course to course to establish continuity for students?
- How might asynchronous assignments like blogs, wikis, and portfolios be integrated and connected throughout the academic program, as tools for reflection and assessment?

Administrators should also consider what types of supplemental support students need in asynchronous online courses. Faculty often serve as the primary point of contact for online students, but they should not be the only point of contact. In an asynchronous course, it can be harder for faculty to get a read on student engagement and needs. Faculty need support and guidance from administrators on how to support students that appear to be uncommunicative or withdrawn in asynchronous courses. The question of online student support is important regardless of the environment, but the extra distance that can arise in asynchronous courses makes it important for administrators to consider. Administrators should reflect the following questions as well.

- Are there virtual resources, including people and programs, where students can go if they are feeling particularly isolated or disconnected in asynchronous courses?
- How do leaders make students aware of these support services?

Administrators should collaborate with faculty to determine how to identify struggling students, and how to connect them with a team of support staff that can provide targeted assistance. Additionally, administrators should think about how they support asynchronous students more broadly, including BIPOC students. Like all asynchronous students, BIPOC students may have limited avenues for connecting with others in the academic program. This feeling will be heightened at institutions with small numbers of non-white students. Administrators must be deliberate in developing services and programs for BIPOC students that address isolation and marginalization and that provide culturally relevant support.

Considerations for Instructional Designers, Faculty Developers, and Support Staff

As faculty developers and instructional designers know, designing an asynchronous course requires attention to detail and support from the learning sciences. In this chapter, I've identified several areas for faculty support that designers and developers are well suited to provide. For example, instructional designers might show faculty how to make the supplemental resources that boost asynchronous engagement, such as introductory welcome videos and voice over screen materials. Instructional designers might also help faculty develop dynamic and technically-enhanced learning scaffolds, ranging from basic graphic organizers to more complex digital and social reading and annotation materials. Topics like facilitating and managing multiple discussion boards simultaneously and incorporating multimedia into boards would be appropriate and beneficial areas for centers for instructional designers to address as well. In terms of professional development, faculty developers might help instructors reflect on asynchronous pedagogy, and help them make strategic decisions about how to incorporate asynchronous tools including quizzes, tests, blogs, and wikis.

 The dearth of literature on both the theory and practice of creating inclusive asynchronous environments that support underrepresented students suggests that designers, developers, CTL staff and administrators can and should be on the vanguard of student support in this important area. These stakeholders should lead conversations and develop training on what inclusion looks like in the context of these schools. Discussions should explore topics related to power and privilege in online classrooms, as well as preempting and responding to micro and macro aggressions. Such offerings are best developed in collaboration with faculty and with students to ensure that they are comprehensive and culturally responsive.

Conclusion

Several collaborative asynchronous learning activities are highlighted in this chapter. Digital social reading and annotation, quizzes, tests, blogs, wikis, podcasts, and portfolios can all help students connect more deeply to the curriculum, to their peers, and to the broader community. Discussion boards, a central part of many online courses, can help students cultivate community in a wide range of ways, including through helping students share more about themselves, engage authentically with peers, work in teams and small groups, and develop shared understanding of course content. Instructors can implement a range of strategies like peer facilitation and role play to increase student interaction in discussion boards. Like synchronous courses, asynchronous courses can be dynamic, interactive learning communities.

5

SYNCHRONOUS TEACHING PRACTICES THAT SUPPORT ONLINE COMMUNITY

Like asynchronous courses, synchronous courses are strengthened when instructors take the time to set the tone for community. While a synchronous course can feel less mysterious than an asynchronous course, instructors still should take the time to prepare students for what to expect in the course, and to address common questions and concerns. While much of this can take place in a synchronous course session, instructors can also consider asynchronously introducing some elements of the course, including the LMS and virtual classroom. Instructors might also review instructional materials and assignments asynchronously. By frontloading this content, instructors can save more of the synchronous time for questions and discussion.

How should instructors allocate synchronous time? Chapter 2 (this volume) noted the importance of cultivating social presence in an online course. Social presence refers to the feelings of connection that occur when authentic sharing takes place. To cultivate social presence in the early days of an online class, students have to get to know their peers and the instructor. In a synchronous class, instructors will have to use class time to help students get to know each other. For students that are new to online learning or at the early stages of an academic program, classroom opportunities for listening to and sharing with peers are invaluable. Synchronous instructors can create formal and informal opportunities for student socialization. For example, instructors might have an informal, "soft start" to synchronous classes, logging in early for students who wish to have a social period. During this time, students can drop in and have casual conversations. These conversations might focus on sports, entertainment, weather, or other general areas of student interest. Berry (2017a) found that online students appreciated the opportunity for "water cooler discussions" at the start of an online class. In an in-person environment, students might naturally coalesce around a water cooler (or over a cup of coffee or during a snack break), such opportunities for informal interaction and discussion are limited in online spaces. Instructors can intentionally recreate these spaces by carving out class time for small talk.

Instructors should also create formal opportunities for online students to interact with peers. Beginning an online session with an icebreaker can pay off dividends in stimulating online students' sense of community. Instructors might ask students to introduce themselves and share their interests, or have students come prepared with a more formal presentation to share with the class. Instructors can also have students bring in other media (songs, pictures, video) to share information about themselves. While the internet is filled with many elaborate ice breakers, icebreakers need not be complicated to be effective. Icebreakers that provide students with space to share their personal, academic and career interests can help support online students' bonds, inside and outside of class. Additionally, instructors who wish to incorporate ice breakers into class sessions throughout the term might have students develop and facilitate some of these activities. Student-facilitation increases student agency in the course, and provides students with an opportunity to share more of themselves with the learning community.

After the Ice is Broken: Organizing a Synchronous Classroom to Support Community

Facilitating a synchronous classroom requires planning and careful attention to detail. Instructors can support students' learning by creating and sharing an agenda for class sessions. A basic agenda for a synchronous class should outline

- topics to be discussed
- materials needed for the session
- time estimates for learning activities
- scheduled breaks

An agenda for a synchronous online class can also note any special instructions for learning activities, particularly those that occur in small/peer-led groups (e.g., breakout rooms). Instructors should consider posting agendas before class so that students have time to review and prepare accordingly.

Creating agendas is one way that instructors can support the needs of diverse learners. Students with disabilities will benefit from the opportunity for advanced preparation, as well as clarity around time on task and break schedules. Sharing break times will also be helpful to students who are managing caregiving responsibilities. Providing a detailed overview of the class can also be beneficial to students who may experience intermittent internet challenges. By ensuring that everyone can participate in the learning environment, agendas support community.

Establishing Norms for Technology Use in Synchronous Classes

As instructors reflect on how they might organize their classrooms, they should also consider what their norms around online participation might be. The "Creating a Safe Environment for all Students" section in chapter 2 (this volume) provides guidance for establishing norms around inclusive class conduct. Those norms are an important baseline for creating a respectful learning environment. Once safety is established, how can instructors create online classrooms that are engaging, interactive, and support community?

At the institutional level, colleges and universities should develop policies and guidelines around expectations for videoconferencing. Instructors may not be able to require students to use video in online classes, but they can highlight the benefits of being on camera for learning and community. These benefits include greater engagement on the part of the student and enhanced connection with peers. Instructors can be honest about the difficulty of teaching to "blank screens," and have students share the benefits of being able to see their peers. Instructors can also note that turning one's camera on can be a self-accountability tool that can promote participation and reduce distraction.

At the same time, instructors should be flexible in regard to their expectations around video. Students might choose to have their cameras off for a variety of reasons, including technology-related challenges. Instructors should be sensitive to this and should not publicly call out students who choose to be off camera. Additionally, instructors should encourage students who choose to be off camera to participate in other ways, such as using the chat function, emoticons, and other engagement methods. In this way, students who are not utilizing video are still involved in the virtual learning community.

One way to increase students' uptake of online video is to create a clear outline of when students should be "on camera" and when cameras might be turned off. Providing students with a clear schedule for breaks and incorporating time off camera into synchronous classes can help students feel more comfortable with time on camera.

Video is not the only online tool that needs to be managed in a synchronous class. In chapter 3 (this volume), the importance of creating clear expectations around the use of the online chat space was noted. The chat can be a beneficial tool for creating community. Chats allow multiple students to participate quickly and simultaneously. Students can use the chat to affirm their peers' comments, ask clarifying questions, and have parallel conversations about the course content. At the same time, chats can be difficult to navigate for some students and instructors, particularly those with visual impairments or processing challenges. Instructors might survey students to find out their feelings about the use of online chat. Instructors can also create some structure around when and how the chat should be used. For example, opening the chat at certain times and closing it at others can make the chat more manageable for all students.

Synchronous instructors must make many decisions about how they will use technology to facilitate connection online. In order to support community, instructors should also make students aware of what their decisions are and how they were made. Additionally, instructors should work with students to develop norms and expectations that meet students' needs. Often, students raise new considerations for teaching and learning that instructors are not aware of. To create online practices around technology use that support community for all students, constant collaboration between students and instructors about needs, expectations, and effective practices is needed.

Teaching in the Synchronous Classroom: Limiting Lecture Time, Increasing Discussion

The flipped classroom is one instructional model that has gotten the attention of educators over the past decade. In a flipped classroom, students engage in independent learning to gain a foundational understanding of core concepts. When students are in synchronous sessions, they work collaboratively on activities that have them synthesize what they have learned by applying and analyzing their core content. In a flipped classroom, students can also strengthen their understanding of new concepts by using class time to evaluate new information together and create new content that reflects what they have learned.

Online learning does not necessarily need to be flipped to be beneficial. However, online instructors should see in flipped learning the significance of an emerging trend in higher education—the shift away from lecture-based formats and toward more interactive modes of learning. Peer interaction is a driving motivation for students that pursue synchronous classes. Toward that end, online instructors must be mindful to not dominate synchronous courses with lecture or other instructor-driven activities. While the perfect mix of instructor-directed and peer-to-peer learning will differ based on the course level and on students' needs, synchronous instructors should be keenly aware of how often they are providing online students with opportunities for participation. The more that students can participate in an online class, the more likely they are to feel engaged, which in turn supports their connections to the course and to community.

Incorporating Asynchronous Learning Activities Into the Synchronous Classroom

While an asynchronous course does not include any synchronous instruction, a synchronous class will typically include some asynchronous learning activities. Students in a synchronous class will be expected to engage with course material in between sessions. For this reason, it is important that synchronous instructors have an understanding of how to create community asynchronously. Focusing on community-building only in synchronous sessions will result in missed opportunities to promote peer interaction, support student bonds, and increase group cohesion.

Instructors can utilize many of the asynchronous strategies outlined in chapters 3 and 4 (this volume) to support community. Asynchronous learning activities like discussion boards, blogs, wikis, podcasts, and portfolios will add value to synchronous online courses. Instructors can also incorporate asynchronous activities into the synchronous session. Having students engage in collaborative reading and writing activities in real time can support student interaction and accelerate the development of the learning community.

Digital social reading and annotation is one asynchronous activity that can be brought into the synchronous classroom. With digital social reading and annotation, students read a shared text, making comments and raising questions as they work collaboratively. Digital social reading and annotation can occur during a synchronous class session, as a way to help manage student collaboration and make student progress visible to the instructor. Used in this way, online instructors can review students' shared assignments and provide instant feedback on student progress. The immediate feedback can increase students' feelings of closeness with peers and with the instructor.

Instructors can also use synchronous online course time for assessment. However, unlike traditional assessments, which are typically independent, graded, and may occur asynchronously, synchronous instructors can utilize collaborative or group assessments as a way to prompt student participation and support community. In a collaborative assessment, students work together to answer questions. Collaborative assessments can help promote a sense of interactivity. They also promote social cohesion and can lead to a greater level of peer understanding. To make collaborative assessments even more interactive, instructors can use polls. Polls give students real-time feedback on their peers' responses and on the correct answer. Being able to see their colleagues' responses, particularly when they are incorrect, creates greater feelings of authenticity and trust. Polls also provide a space for affirmation of students' perspectives and are an opportunity to create shared understanding. In all of these ways, using polls or other tools for collaborative assessment can support community.

Instructors can also use synchronous time to have students engage in collaborative writing. Working together in shared documents, students can develop written work that reflects their understanding of course content. Instructors can take an active role in students shared writing, using technology to monitor student activity in real time and give feedback. Having students engage in collaborative writing also ensures that they have a scaffold for any asynchronous writing activities.

Discussion boards can be used in between classes to continue to facilitate peer-to-peer interaction and to support continued reflection and learning in between synchronous sessions. As noted in chapter 4 (this volume), there are a range of strategies instructors can use to make discussion board participation more community-oriented. Peer facilitation and role play are great tools for encouraging interactivity and promoting online community-building. Synchronous class sessions allow instructors to model these learning techniques for students.

Instructors who use discussion boards in between synchronous sessions should take care to incorporate students' discussion board content into the synchronous sessions. Instructors can use the boards to spark discussion, provide clarification, or correct common misunderstandings. When students see that their responses will be used to support learning and scaffold synchronous discussion, engagement will deepen.

Incorporating traditionally asynchronous elements into a synchronous course is one way to support community in online courses. However, there are also many synchronous elements that instructors can leverage to promote community. Strategies for doing so are outlined in the sections that follow.

What Should Students Do in a Synchronous Class? Learning Activities, Synchronous Courses, and Project Management

One unique asset of the synchronous class is that it provides a space for project management and project development. Students meeting in real time can develop presentations and multimedia (videos and podcasts) and practice presentations. Instructors can also support students in developing project management plans for completing tasks in between synchronous sessions. By providing students with the opportunity to work together to create shared meaning, synchronous courses support students' sense of community.

Student Facilitation in Synchronous Courses

Another way to deepen the community-building opportunities of synchronous classes is to let students lead. Facilitating a learning activity or class session can be empowering for all students, as they have an opportunity to develop leadership skills and share more deeply with peers. For underrepresented and historically marginalized students, course facilitation can give them an opportunity to shift course discussion and learning activities. Student facilitation also supports engagement, deepens understanding, and provides new opportunities for students to bond with each other. Because of its' benefits, student facilitation should be a regular component of the online course.

There are many activities students can facilitate. Students can

- summarize course readings
- teach selected material
- present new material to the class
- facilitate a discussion
- moderate a debate
- give peers feedback

Student facilitation is most effective when instructors carefully scaffold and organize the learning task. Before having students facilitate, instructors should clearly define their expectations, modeling when possible. Depending on the task and the academic level, instructors might consider using rubrics or other assessment tools to help students meet expectations.

Collaborative Learning Activities for Synchronous Courses

General online collaborative learning activities were highlighted in chapter 2 (this volume). In a synchronous classroom, instructors have the opportunity to go even deeper with collaboration, leveraging the real-time aspect of the class to create dynamic discussions and peer interactions. Many common activities for in-person classes lend nicely to the online format.

Synchronous Collaborative Learning Activity #1: Think-Pair-Share

In a think-pair-share, students begin by approaching a learning task independently. After a preestablished period, students work in pairs to discuss their answer and to generate deeper understanding of the learning activity. After another preestablished period of time, students share their ideas with the larger group. A think-pair-share is a simple way to ensure that all students are participating. Students, particularly those who are shyer, will appreciate the opportunity for both independent and small group reflection. The scaffolded nature of think-pair-share can support students' feelings of trust and belonging in the learning environment.

Synchronous Collaborative Learning Activity #2: Fishbowl

A fishbowl is a learning activity that supports structured discussion among medium- and large-sized groups. A few members of the group are selected to be in a "fishbowl," the inner circle of participants. This group will discuss a topic for a timed period, and the larger group observes and takes notes. The instructor might act as moderator for the inner circle, to add more structure to the discussion. After the time period has ended, the participants in the outer circle can comment or ask questions of the inner circle participants. The structured nature of a fishbowl can add depth and clarity to student learning. Additionally, like a think-pair-share, the assigned roles of the fishbowl activity ensure that all students are participating. Fishbowls can be used to help students organize thoughts, create shared meaning, and establish consensus, which are all important elements of community-building.

Synchronous Collaborative Learning Activity #3: Case Study

In a case study analysis, students analyze a real-world problem and attempt to provide a response or solution to it. Students are typically provided with a prompt that outlines the problem or challenge, as well as data to provide context. This data can include videos, audio, or quotes articulating the experiences of different stakeholders, as well as charts, graphs, and other quantitative data to highlight a problem. Depending on the course, students can be asked to develop an answer to the question, problem, or prompt, or develop a more detailed response, such as an action plan or proposal.

Case study analysis helps students develop problem-solving and statistical-reasoning skills and builds their capacity for complex decision-making and group participation. Additionally, the real-world focus of case study analysis will be beneficial for students. As with the aforementioned tasks, working together to create shared meaning helps students develop a sense of community.

Synchronous Collaborative Learning Activity #4: Problem-Based or Project-Based Learning

Project-based learning (PBL), during which students work on a task over an extended period of time, was introduced in chapter 2 (this volume). Incorporating PBL into synchronous sessions can be a way to add structure to student work time. When tasks are clearly delineated and expectations are outlined, students can work together in a more productive and meaningful way. Online students might also appreciate having class time dedicated to group work, so that they spend less time coordinating with peers asynchronously. Synchronous instruction can also be used for problem-based learning, during which students are asked to apply a set of skills, strategies, and problem-solving techniques to answer certain questions. Problem-based learning lends itself to all subjects, but particularly to areas like math, science, technology, and other fields that require clear sets of discrete skills. Effective problems for problem-based learning require students to search for information, consider multiple solutions, and engage in dialogue and complex decision-making. Problems can be solved over the course of a session or over the course of the instructional term.

Managing the Collaborative Learning Space: Teaching Strategies for Breakout Rooms

One of the most important features of a synchronous online classroom is the breakout room. Breakout rooms allow instructors to split apart large groups of students, allowing them to work in small groups and teams. Because breakout rooms allow for more intimate groupings of students, they can support increased student collaboration and provide a space for deeper, more authentic peer-to-peer learning. However, creating a productive space requires more than the click of a button. Breakout rooms require management and planning to be effective. Strategies for managing breakout rooms include

- saving time for preassigning groups
- developing clear expectations for group participation

- assigning students roles for the breakout rooms
- frequently monitoring student progress

Save Time By Preassigning Groups

Assigning students to breakout groups can be tedious and time consuming. Many Web-conferencing software programs allow for the creation of random groups, which saves time and increases the variety of groups. Some systems allow instructors to preassign groups, so that the work of sorting students is not done during the class. Preassigning groups allows instructors to create more balanced groups, especially as they consider factors like student skill, ability, interest, and diversity.

Develop Clear Expectations for Group Participation

It is important to have clear guidelines for all learning activities. In addition to outlining the logistics of the group (membership, duration, etc.), instructors should be sure that the task is clearly defined. Some core questions to answer in developing a breakout task include:

- What are students supposed to do in the breakout rooms?
- Is there a question to answer or an assignment to complete?
- How will completion be assessed? Will students have to complete an "exit ticket" or other indicator of participation?

Instructors should also provide asynchronous access to instructions, in the event that students get disconnected from the breakout room or from the synchronous session. Written instructions for breakout room participation should be provided in a shared space. Some virtual classrooms allow you to share files in the live session. While this is very helpful, instructors should consider posting the instructions to the LMS as well. Instructors might share complex assignments before class, so that students can review them and ask questions in class. Instructors can also consider posting them on the LMS so that students have access. If the task is complex or has multiple parts, instructors might encourage students to review it before class and come to the session with questions.

Assign Students Roles for the Breakout Rooms

Another strategy for developing clear expectations for breakout group participation is to assign roles. Instructors must have a structure for teamwork (Saltz & Heckman, 2020). One way to structure breakouts is to use a scripted approach, where each student in the group has a particular role with clear responsibilities. Roles can be task-oriented (e.g., note taker, moderator, reporter), or more cognitively oriented (e.g., discussion starter, discussion skeptic, discussion wrapper; Olesova et al., 2016). Saltz and Heckman (2020) experimented with the roles in a computer science classroom, using a structured pair activity (SPA) model. In an SPA, two members of a pair have clearly defined roles. In this case study, the roles were driver and observer. The driver was tasked with completing a coding goal, and the observer was tasked with evaluating the drivers' work for accuracy. The observer also was responsible for connecting the drivers' work to a larger assignment. The observer would wait until the driver was done to provide feedback, and students would switch roles every 15 minutes. Saltz and Heckman (2020) contrasted this process with unstructured pair work, and found that students in a structured pair demonstrated increased engagement and improved productivity. This model also facilitated student bonding, as students expressed interest in continuing to work with their pairs on future projects. However, there were some challenges. Rotating in 15-minute intervals was difficult and did not always happen. Instructors must factor in how much a particular task might take, as well as any technical components that might slow down a transition. Still, most teams quickly adapted, developing an interval for switching that worked for their project.

Depending on the student population, a scripted approach may be unnecessary. Some students will have their own working dynamics that lend to productivity. Saltz and Heckman (2020) note that scripts might interfere with more organic or exploratory thinking. Assigned roles can become stale if they are not frequently rotated. Instructors should vary role play based on the needs of their students.

Frequently Monitor Student Progress

Monitoring student participation in breakout rooms can support student engagement and success. Students will be less inclined to get off task if they believe an instructor will be present at some point in the activity. All students, and particularly those who are struggling, will benefit from an active instructor who is readily available to answer questions that arise in different breakout groups. In a face-to-face classroom, an instructor would simply walk between groups of students, answering questions as they come up. In a virtual classroom, monitoring student participation in breakout rooms takes more coordination (Saltz & Heckman, 2020). Instructors will have to intentionally move between each room. This might be cumbersome and time consuming, depending on the Web conferencing software and on instructors' technical proficiency. If instructors have a teaching assistant, they can provide support by participating in a breakout room. Another way to make monitoring student progress easier in breakout rooms is to consider having students use a shared document to demonstrate their participation. Shared documents will update in real time, allowing instructors to see participation in different groups. Instructors might use the document to support classroom management, entering into the rooms of groups who aren't making progress in the shared document.

Considerations for Underrepresented and Historically Marginalized Students

Many of the synchronous strategies outlined have centered on student collaboration. While collaboration is essential to supporting connection and facilitating community, instructors should be mindful of the ways in which broader social dynamics can impact and undermine student interaction. Students from historically underrepresented and marginalized groups may find that the same microaggressions they experience in the broader society are present in the classroom. While the ways in which these instances play out will vary significantly based on context, instructors must be mindful of the fact that they can occur. Instructors should frequently check in with students, both as groups and as individuals, to learn about how collaborative activities are going and to address any challenges that can occur. Additionally, instructors must do their due diligence to ensure that activities do not overly privilege students with strong oral communication skills. They should also ensure that activities don't rely so much on speaking that they inadvertently disadvantage students who may lack strong verbal skills, including international students, second-language learners, and students with disabilities. One way to ensure that every student has an opportunity to participate in a learning task is by giving each group member a unique role.

With planning, instructors can also ensure that their collaborative spaces are more equitable for all students. By clearly assigning students roles for assignments, and holding individual students accountable for fulfilling these roles, instructors decrease the likelihood that any one student is overburdened in a group activity. Instructors should also take an active role in groups so that they can become aware of any dynamics and proactively address emergent challenges.

Accessibility is a vital component of an equitable and inclusive classroom. Synchronous learning may present many challenges for students with disabilities. Visually impaired students may be asked to make sense of multiple files simultaneously, which can be difficult. Hearing impaired students may face challenges navigating discussions where closed captioning is not used (or is not accurate), or in discussions which are not well-facilitated and include multiple speakers speaking at the same time. Instructors should be mindful to think about accessibility not just in terms of course materials, but in terms of course facilitation as well.

Instructors should also be aware of accessibility challenges that might emerge as a result of sudden changes in learning activities or delivery methods. Additionally, the use of tools outside of the LMS, either by instructors or by student-facilitators, can create accessibility challenges. Instructors will want to check with disability services and instructional designers on campus to make sure that materials that are brought into the learning space comply with accessibility guidelines.

Additionally, online instructors must include accessibility in their planning for small-group and student-led activities as well. Just as instructors typically design online courses around accessibility guidelines, students should be expected to participate and facilitate activities in ways that are accessible to the entire class.

Considerations for Administrators

This chapter challenges some of the commonly held beliefs around synchronous learning. Just because a course is synchronous does not mean that student engagement will naturally occur. Instructors must create and maximize opportunities for connection in synchronous online courses. This chapter provides strategies for facilitating students' social and academic interactions. Administrators should keep these strategies in mind as they support and evaluate faculty. Administrators should also consider how they can provide professional learning and guidance to faculty who need support in moving beyond lecture and toward more interactive online teaching. While direct instruction is important, successful online instructors will likely utilize more student-led activities than instructor-led activities. Administrators should support and incentivize the use of teaching strategies that promote peer-to-peer interaction.

This chapter also highlights the necessity of focusing on accessibility in every facet of synchronous course planning and facilitation. Because synchronous courses provide many opportunities for interaction, they can present many challenges for inclusion of students with various learning needs. Administrators must support faculty in being aware of the specific challenges that their students face, and provide training, resources, and other support for meeting student and faculty needs in the areas of accessibility and disability support.

Considerations for Instructional Designers, Faculty Developers, and Support Staff

Instructional designers, faculty developers, and support staff can be a vital asset to instructors who are learning to teach in the complex, multifaceted context that is the synchronous classroom. These stakeholders are well-positioned to help faculty with their virtual facilitation skills. Supporting instructors in managing multiple facets of the online class simultaneously will be beneficial to faculty and will promote better learning outcomes for students. A key area of the virtual classroom where online faculty may need support is in the area of facilitating and managing multiple learning environments (e.g., breakout rooms) at once. Some instructors shy away from breakout rooms because they cannot manage all learners simultaneously. Professional learning opportunities that focus on managing multiple groups can help increase the likelihood that instructors will effectively incorporate breakout rooms into their teaching practice.

Some instructors may be comfortable with technology generally, but may struggle when incorporating interactive learning activities into their online classes. Support staff can help faculty develop and implement interactive ice breakers, learning activities, and class projects that promote engagement and support community.

Support staff can also help instructors think through accessibility-related concerns, particularly when it comes to collaborative and student-led activities. While faculty typically have the opportunity to get feedback on their course materials from support staff, students may not have that option. Additionally, students lack access to training that could support them in accessible teaching and facilitation. If online instructors expect students to facilitate portions of synchronous courses, then institutions should provide students with the resources needed to support accessible facilitation.

Conclusion

The embedded opportunity for instructor-student and peer-to-peer interaction is one of the most vital assets of a synchronous course. Instructors can build on this opportunity by intentionally creating opportunities for connection and collaboration. As synchronous instructors move away from lecture-based teaching and toward student-driven instruction, they can use tools like breakout rooms, and activities like student facilitation, think-pair-share, fishbowl, case studies, and problem/PBL to help facilitate community in synchronous classes.

CONCLUSION

This book has offered a rich and expansive way for educators to think about online teaching and learning. The book separates out concepts that are often viewed in aggregate. By looking at online learning by modality, synchronous, asynchronous, and hybrid, the book allows educators to consider online learning with greater depth and complexity. Additionally, this sharpened focus allows educators to see with greater clarity the challenges that diverse learners might experience in these settings, and how educators might skillfully help students overcome these challenges. This book also calls educators to look upon the technologies used in online courses with greater nuance. Rather than viewing tools as simply helpful or not helpful, this work asks readers to consider how and why certain elements of the LMS or virtual classroom might support students' experiences. The critical perspectives put forth in this work empower educators to make informed choices that serve a broad array of students.

Additionally, this work has offered educators a more integrated and holistic way to think about online courses and programs. Berry's integrated framework for community in online courses and programs reminds educators of the need to consider students experiences both at the classroom level and at the institutional level. In so doing, this framework widens the sphere of practitioners that influence online learners' experiences. By looking at online experiences at the course and program level, education leaders can think beyond the individual instructor, and consider the ecosystem of practitioners that support the instructor, including instructional designers, faculty developers, and information technology staff. Additionally, educators can use this expanded perspective to consider online students' experiences beyond the classroom. The framework and the book as a whole call for a greater integration of support professionals, including student affairs staff, into research and practice on online learning.

Perhaps the greatest contribution of this work is its' focus on community as a frame. As noted throughout the book, community is an experience that is affective, and therefore, subjective. Because it is subjective, educators must continue to give detailed consideration to community in all of its nuances, including modality and course format. Educators must also consider the ways in which different identity characteristics add greater nuance to students' experiences of community, including race, sex, class, and ability. Additionally, practitioners must also be mindful that community is as much a social and emotional concept as it is an academic one. Given the increasing cultural attention to issues of student mental health and wellness, frameworks like community, which consider the social and emotional aspects of teaching and learning, are highly relevant.

As readers continue to ponder the concepts outlined in this book, I hope that they will leave with a renewed commitment toward looking at topics of diversity, equity, and inclusion in online classrooms. This work asks readers to consider the ways in which racism, sexism, classism, and ableism can occur in online courses and programs. These considerations should be a starting point for future discussions and action. As noted throughout the book, there is a dearth of scholarship on these topics. As such, it is incumbent upon practitioners, including readers of this book, to reflect on, test out, and document the strategies that they use to better serve historically marginalized and underrepresented populations. In the interim, this book serves as a starting point for a more inclusive agenda on online teaching and learning.

This book has provided educators, administrators, and support staff with important guidance on how to cultivate an online community. Stakeholders should use these strategies in their respective contexts, altering them to meet the unique needs of their students. Online students do have unique needs, and these needs can vary based on a number of identity-related characteristics, including race, sex, gender, sexual orientation, socioeconomic status, and ability or disability. This book provides a starting point for educators to consider the ways in which diversity emerges in online courses and programs, and how they might respond to the needs of historically marginalized and underrepresented students with support and cultural sensitivity. As educators become more aware of this truth, that online students are diverse and have diverse needs, the strategies used to support historically marginalized and underrepresented learners will grow. For now, this work provides a broad base from which to consider the needs of different learners in online courses. Educators can use this book as a springboard for supporting and engaging a broad and diverse cross-section of online students.

The COVID-19 pandemic forced institutions around the world to consider how online learning might fit into their instructional delivery plans. As a result of this process, age-old debates about online learning were revived. Chief among them was whether or not it was possible to create community in an online course. This book suggests that not only is it possible, it is critical for educators to create dynamic, inclusive, and engaging online learning communities. By helping students create community—spaces where students experience feelings of membership, trust, and belonging within a supportive social group, educators can improve students' academic performance and support their social and emotional well-being.

APPENDIX A

Cultivating Community During a Pandemic

Online Teaching, Emergency Remote Instruction, and Pandemic Pedagogy

The COVID-19 pandemic placed renewed attention to the importance of emotional well-being and community in higher education. The stress of the transition from in-person instruction to remote teaching, as well as the greater uncertainty around health and economic stability placed additional stress on students, faculty, and staff. A report conducted in the summer of 2020 found that one third of students in undergraduate, graduate, and professional schools had depression, anxiety, or both (Chirikov et al., 2020). This report, which included data from 30,725 undergraduates and 15,346 graduate and professional students also found that mental health disorders were "most pronounced" for low-income, LGBTQ, female, and BIPOC students. In order to provide social and emotional support to students, many institutions also increased extracurricular virtual offerings. These offerings include counseling and emotional support, as well as social activities to help preserve a sense of continuity, strengthen student bonds, and provide some stress relief.

Many institutions that were temporarily online due to the pandemic have planned on returning to some form of in-person instruction. However, the pandemic and the sudden shift for online learning have important implications for educators and administrators. First, it is important to note that there is a difference between online courses, which were intentionally designed to be online, and emergency remote teaching.

Hodges et al. (2020) wrote,

> In contrast to experiences that are planned from the beginning and designed to be online, emergency remote teaching (ERT) is a temporary shift of instructional delivery to an alternate delivery mode due to crisis circumstances. The primary objective in these circumstances is not to re-create a robust educational ecosystem but rather to provide temporary access to instruction and instructional supports in a manner that is quick to set up and is reliably available during an emergency or crisis. (p. 2)

Unlike online courses, which are deliberately planned for online delivery, emergency classes arise rapidly due to fluid, often unpredictable contexts (e.g., natural disasters, disease outbreak, etc.). In such contexts, instructors may only have days, even hours, to prepare. Gacs et al., (2020) argued that emergency remote teaching is not truly online teaching, but online triage. As a result, some of the typical quality markers of online courses may not be attended to, in the interest of rapidly transferring the course to a digital format. It is important to note that issues of accessibility should always be considered in sudden shifts to delivery. Instructors might seek support from disability support services, instructional design teams, and their center for teaching and learning to ensure that a transition to emergency remote instruction is accessible to all students.

The 2020 pandemic brought a global focus to the need to plan for emergency online course preparation and implementation. When placing a course online in an emergency situation, there are a few things instructors should consider. One is ease of access to information. Whether you are using a course web page or an LMS, it is important for students to be able to easily find relevant information, particularly in a crisis. Web pages with too many folders or files can be confusing to the students. Instructors should pursue streamlined, highly organized designs for course websites. Additionally, instructors might consider what their course looks like from a mobile device. In fluid situations (e.g., natural disasters), students' typical workspaces can be inaccessible. This might increase students' reliance on mobile technologies to access courses. Instructors should ensure that course webpages are optimized for mobile devices.

Emergency remote instruction requires rapid adaptation. However, instructors should be careful in how they modify their courses for a virtual format. Instructors may jump to using popular tools in times of crisis because they seem easy to access or simple to use. Such decisions should be made in conjunction with institutional leadership. This will increase the likelihood that the tools used meet the university's guides for technology security, and that the tools comply with accessibility needs and mandates. Additionally, tools approved by the university are more likely to sync to a central source, which is important for learning management.

Another consideration for emergency remote instruction is to consider the flexibility of the instructional delivery method. Here, there are be some tradeoffs that instructors should consider. For example, synchronous courses might be beneficial in moments of difficulty, as they allow the opportunity to create a shared space for emotional support. However, synchronous sessions might be difficult for students during a time of crisis, as some students will be experiencing emerging challenges in real time. Instructors should consider the unique needs of their student population when deciding on a format for their emergency remote course. To make synchronous courses more accessible, instructors might consider recording them, so that students who cannot attend in real time can still have access to the information. Asynchronous sessions can offer students more flexibility and might seem like a better choice in a time of sudden crisis. While the flexibility of asynchronous teaching is a definite benefit, be aware that some students might find the sudden switch from synchronous to asynchronous learning unsettling. Instructors might consider a synchronous option for students who desire it, with asynchronous components for those who might find synchronous learning inaccessible due to an evolving situation.

When adapting a course due to an emergency, instructors should consider the social and emotional needs of their students. One way to do this is to consider scaling back the workload to reflect students' (and instructors) diminished capacity for productivity due to the crisis. Another way to do this is to create space for students to express their feelings related to the crisis. This might include creating a synchronous session during or after classes for students to share their feelings. At minimum, it should include sharing any campus resources for mental health.

By preparing for emergency remote teaching; faculty, staff, and administrators can increase the likelihood that academic continuity will be maintained in a crisis. Additionally, crisis planning supports social cohesion during an emergency event, which will likely be stressful and unsettling for students and instructors. By attending to the aforementioned, educators can increase the likelihood that students' academic and social needs for clarity, support, and connection are met. This level of support will, in turn, increase online students' sense of community.

University administrators should also consider the social and emotional needs of faculty and staff during a crisis. In a natural disaster, faculty may experience challenges related to housing and physical or mental health. The COVID-19 pandemic has presented mental health challenges for Americans across the board. A CDC report released in May 2020 said that one third of Americans were dealing with symptoms of anxiety and depression (CDC, 2021). The challenges that the pandemic has placed on life broadly and higher education institutions specifically have increased the risk of burnout among faculty. According to the World Health Organization (2019), burnout results from "chronic workplace stress that has not been successfully managed" (para. 4). Increased stressors in the workplace, caused by the rapid shift to online learning and fears over safe reopening, and increased stressors around the workplace related to childcare, health, and safety, can all contribute to burnout. When faculty members experience burnout, they are more likely to see a decline in performance, and an increase in difficult physical and mental health challenges. To help support faculty and staff with burnout, administrators can consider acknowledging the challenges presented by the crisis at hand, streamlining and reducing expectations, and developing structures and processes that are respectful of individuals' childcare and personal needs (Gruber et al., 2020).

The COVID-19 pandemic of 2020 has also brought attention to the need for what some have called "pandemic pedagogy," a flexible, sensitive, and holistic way to provide education during a pandemic (Milman, 2020). In addition to bringing about the shifts that are typical in other types of crises (e.g., the need for remote instruction, stresses associated with responding to the immediate aftermath of a crisis, and prolonged challenges to mental and financial health), the pervasiveness of a pandemic creates an added layer of stress. Everyone is impacted, albeit not equally. Still, the overarching nature of the pandemic, and the uncertainty surrounding it, requires instructors and administrators to be particularly mindful of their choices around instructional delivery during this time.

Milman (2020) and others offer several tips for implementing pandemic pedagogy. Accepting that the situation is highly fluid, instructors should communicate frequently and honestly with their students. Instructors should prioritize students' needs, as well as their own. This may mean streamlining the course and reducing content temporarily, to reduce stress. Certain assignments will no longer be feasible, and expectations of a certain level of student output should be altered. Instructors should be honest with themselves about the capacity they and their students have to persist in the face of the emergent challenge. If possible, instructors should create routines and schedules for students. These routines will look different than the routines implemented prior to the pandemic. For example, an instructor might set up routine virtual office hours meetings, to allow students a space to check in. The instructor might send a weekly email to help students organize their thoughts around the course. Consistency can be a powerful tool in helping students and instructors manage the stress of teaching through a difficult time. Instructors and administrators should also collaborate with a diverse set of community members to make decisions about instructional delivery. This will increase the likelihood that decisions are feasible, as well as culturally and contextually relevant to the population that the university serves. Finally, instructors might consider contingency plans for teaching and learning, should they or their students become ill during the pandemic. Even as the pandemic becomes less of an acute challenge, the concept of pandemic pedagogy provides a strong model for instructors and administrators who are seeking to navigate any fluid, unexpected crisis. The focus on streamlining communication, providing social and emotional support for students, and having clear and consistent points of contact for students will be helpful in a range of crises, and increase students' sense of community.

REFERENCES

Abes, E. S., & Wallace, M. M. (2018). "People see me, but they don't see me": An intersectional study of college students with physical disabilities. *Journal of College Student Development, 59*(5), 545–562. http://doi.org/10.1353/csd.2018.0052

Akcaoglu, M., & Lee, E. (2016, April). Increasing social presence in online learning through small group discussions. *The International Review of Research in Open and Distributed Learning, 17*(3), 1–17. https://files.eric.ed.gov/fulltext/EJ1102673.pdf

Aloni, M. (2016, October). *The effect of discussion role assignments on students' perceptions of the effectiveness of class discussions* [Paper presentation]. Annual Conference on Teaching of the Society for the Teaching of Psychology, Atlanta, GA.

Annamma, S. A., Ferri, B. A., & Connor, D. J. (2018). Disability critical race theory: Exploring the intersectional lineage, emergence, and potential futures of DisCrit in education. *Review of Research in Education, 42*(1), 46–71. https://doi.org/10.3102/0091732X18759041

Association of American Colleges and Universities. (2021, April 29). *Making excellence inclusive*. AAC&U. https://www.aacu.org/making-excellence-inclusive

Athens, W. (2018). Perceptions of the persistent: Engagement and learning community in underrepresented populations. *Online Learning, 22*(2), 27–57. https://files.eric.ed.gov/fulltext/EJ1181406.pdf

Atwater, C., Borup, J., Baker, R., & West, R. E. (2017). Student perceptions of video communication in an online sport and recreation studies graduate course. *Sport Management Education Journal, 11*(1), 3–12. https://doi.org/10.1007/s11423-019-09709-9

Baker, R., Dee, T., Evans, B., & John, J. (2018). *Bias in online classes: Evidence from a field experiment* (CEPA Working Paper No. 18-03). Stanford Center for Education Policy Analysis. http://cepa.stanford.edu/wp18-03

Balaji, M. S., & Chakrabarti, D. (2010). Student interactions in online discussion forum: Empirical research from 'media richness theory' perspective. *Journal of Interactive Online learning, 9*(1), 1–22. https://www.academia.edu/50636530/Student_Interactions_In_Online_Discussion_Forum_Empirical_Research_From_Media_Richness_TheoryPerspective

Bensimon, E. M., & Malcolm, L. E. (Eds.). (2012). *Confronting equity issues on campus: Implementing the equity scorecard in theory and practice*. Stylus.

Berry, S. (2017a). Building community in online doctoral classrooms: Instructor practices that support community. *Online Learning Journal, 21*(2). https://olj.onlinelearningconsortium.org/index.php/olj/article/view/875/265

Berry, S. (2017b). *Exploring community in an online doctoral program: A digital case study* (Doctoral dissertation, University of Southern California).

Berry, S. (2018a). Building community in an online graduate program: Exploring the role of an in-person orientation. *The Qualitative Report, 23*(7), 1673–1687. https://nsuworks.nova.edu/tqr/vol23/iss7/13

Berry, S. (2018b). Professional development for online faculty: Instructors' perspectives on cultivating technical, pedagogical and content knowledge in a distance program. *Journal of Computing in Higher Education, 31*(1): 121–136. https://doi.org/10.1007/s12528-018-9194-0

Berry, S. (2019a). Teaching to connect: Community-building strategies for the virtual classroom. *Online Learning, 23*(1), 164–183. https://doi.org/10.24059/olj.v23i1.1425

Berry, S. (2019b). The role of video and text chat in a virtual classroom: How technology impacts community. In J. Yoon & P. Semingson (Eds.), *Educational technology and resources for synchronous learning in higher education* (pp. 173–187). IGI Global.

Blakeney, A. M. (2005). Antiracist pedagogy: Definition, theory, and professional development. *Journal of Curriculum and Pedagogy, 2*(1), 119–132.

Bower, M. (2008). Affordance analysis—matching learning tasks with learning technologies. *Educational Media International, 45*(1), 3–15. http://dx.doi.org/10.1080/09523980701847115

Brown, S. K., & Burdsal, C. A. (2012). An exploration of sense of community and student success using the national survey of student engagement. *The Journal of General Education, 61*(4), 433–460. https://doi.org/10.5325/jgeneeduc.61.4.0433

Carlen, U., & Jobring, O. (2005). The rationale of online learning communities. *International Journal of Web-Based Communities, 1*(3), 272–295. https://citeseerx.ist.psu.edu/viewdoc/download?doi=10.1.1.599.7386&rep=rep1&type=pdf

Center for Urban Education. (2020). Equity-minded inquiry series: Syllabus Review. Rossier School of Education, University of Southern California. https://static1.squarespace.com/static/5eb5c03682a92c5f96da4fc8/t/5f3a1ad2dd13385c2b4e76bd/1597643493581/Syllabus+Review_Summer2020.pdf

Centers for Disease Control and Prevention. (2021, October 20). *Anxiety and depression: Household pulse survey*. https://www.cdc.gov/nchs/covid19/pulse/mental-health.htm

Chen, Y., Lei, J., & Cheng, J. (2019). What if online students take on the responsibility: Students' cognitive presence and peer facilitation techniques. *Online Learning, 23*(1), 37–61. https://doi.org/10.24059/olj.v23i1.1348

Chirikov, I., Soria, K. M., Horgos, B., & Jones-White, D. (2020). *Undergraduate and graduate students' mental health during the COVID-19 pandemic*. SERU Consortium, University of California–Berkeley, and University of Minnesota. https://cshe.berkeley.edu/seru-covid-survey-reports

Clark, C., Strudler, N., & Grove, K. (2015). Comparing asynchronous and synchronous video vs. text-based discussions in an online teacher education course. *Online Learning*, *19*(3), 48–69. https://files.eric.ed.gov/fulltext/EJ1067484.pdf

Collins, P. H. (1986). Learning from the outsider within: The sociological significance of Black feminist thought. *Social Problems*, *33*(6), s14–s32.

Cottom, T. M. (2015) "Who do you think you are?" When marginality meets academic microcelebrity. *ADA: A Journal of Gender, New Media, and Technology*, *7*. https://doi.org/10.1177/1461444818781324

Crenshaw, K. (1990). Mapping the margins: Intersectionality, identity politics, and violence against women of color. *Stanford Law Review*, *43*, 1241.

Dennen, V. P. (2005). From message posting to learning dialogues: Factors affecting learner participation in asynchronous discussion. *Distance Education*, *26*(1), 127–148. https://doi.org/10.1080/01587910500081376

De Wever, B., Van Keer, H., Schellens, T., & Valcke, M. (2009). Structuring asynchronous discussion groups: The impact of role assignment and self-assessment on students' levels of knowledge construction through social negotiation. *Journal of Computer Assisted Learning*, *25*(2), 177–188. https://doi.org/10.1111/j.1365-2729.2008.00292.x

de Wit, H. (2013, June 1). COIL: Virtual mobility without commercialisation. *University World News*. https://www.universityworldnews.com/post.php?story=20130528175741647

DiAngelo, R. (2018). *White fragility: Why it's so hard for White people to talk about racism*. Beacon Press.

Faucher, C., Jackson, M., & Cassidy, W. (2014). Cyberbullying among university students: Gendered experiences, impacts, and perspectives. *Education Research International*, *2014*(1), 1–10. https://www.researchgate.net/publication/286281436_Cyberbullying_among_University_Students_Gendered_Experiences_Impacts_and_Perspectives

Federal Communications Commission. (2020). *2020 Broadband deployment report. Broadband progress reports*. (FCC Publication No. FCC 20-50). Federal Communications Commission. https://www.fcc.gov/reports-research/reports/broadband-progress-reports/2020-broadband-deployment-report

Foushee, R. D. (2018). Breaking free: The benefits of non-expository, low-stakes writing assignments in psychology courses. In T. L. Kuther (Ed.), *Integrating writing into the college classroom: Strategies for promoting student skills*. Society for the Teaching of Psychology.

Fovet, F. (2020, July). *Examining the (lack of) impact the #disabilitytoowhite movement has had on higher ed disability service provision*. Pacific Rim International Conference on Disability and Diversity Conference Proceedings. Honolulu, Hawai'i: Center on Disability Studies, University of Hawai'i at Mānoa.

Fox, J., Cruz, C., & Lee, J. Y. (2015) Perpetuating online sexism offline: Anonymity, interactivity, and the effects of sexist hashtags on social media. *Computers in Human Behavior*, *52*, 436–442. https://doi.org/10.1016/j.chb.2015.06.024

Gacs, A., Goertler, S., Spasova, S. (2020). Planned online language education versus crisis-prompted online language teaching: Lessons for the future. *Foreign Language Annals*, *53*(2), 380–392. https://doi.org/10.1111/flan.12460

Garrison, D. R. (2012). Article review: Social presence within the community of inquiry framework. *The International Review of Research in Open and Distributed Learning, 13*(1), 250–253. https://doi.org/10.19173/irrodl.v13i1.1184

Garrison, D. R., Anderson, T., & Archer, W. (2001). Critical thinking, cognitive presence, and computer conferencing in distance education. *American Journal of Distance Education, 15*(1), 7–23. https://doi.org/10.1080/08923640109527071

Gedera, D. (2014). Students' experiences of learning in a virtual classroom: An activity theory perspective. *International Journal of Education and Development Using ICT, 10*(4), 93–101. https://files.eric.ed.gov/fulltext/EJ1059024.pdf

Gopalan, M., & Brady, S. T. (2020). College students' sense of belonging: A national perspective. *Educational Researcher, 49*(2), 134–137. https://doi.org/10.3102/0013189X19897622

Gruber, J., Prinstein, M. J., Clark, L. A., Rottenberg, J., Abramowitz, J. S., Albano, A. M., Aldao, A., Borelli, J. L., Chung, T., Davila, J., Forbes, E. E., Gee, D. G., Hall, G. C., Nagayama, H., Hallion, L. S., Hinshaw, S. P., Hoffman, S. G., Hollon, S. D., Joormann, J. . . . & Weinstock, L. M. (2020). Mental health and clinical psychological science in the time of COVID-19: Challenges, opportunities, and a call to action. *American Psychologist, 76*(3), 409–426. https://doi.org/10.1037/amp0000707

Guillermo-Wann, C., Hurtado, S., & Ruiz Alvarado, A. (2015). Creating inclusive environments: The mediating effect of faculty and staff validation on the relationship of discrimination/bias to students' sense of belonging. *Journal Committed to Social Change on Race and Ethnicity, 1*(1), 60–80. https://doi.org/10.15763/issn.2642-2387.2015.1.1.59-81

Harrington, C., & Aloni, M. (2013, June 1). *Promoting critical thinking through online discussion: Developing questions and managing conversations* [Paper presentation]. Lilly Conference on College and University Teaching and Learning, Bethesda, MD.

Henderson, M., & Phillips, M. (2015). Video-based feedback on student assessment: Scarily personal. *Australasian Journal of Educational Technology, 31*(1), 51–66. https://doi.org/10.14742/ajet.1878

Hess, A. (2017, June 14). *Why women aren't welcome on the internet.* Pacific Standard. https://psmag.com/why-women-aren-t-welcome-on-the-internet-aa21fdbc8d6

Howell, G. S., LaCour, M. M., & McGlawn, P. A. (2017). Constructing student knowledge in the online classroom: The effectiveness of focal prompts. *College Student Journal, 51*(4), 483–490. link.gale.com/apps/doc/A519935683/AONE?u=callutheran&sid=googleScholar&xid=e509dae4

Hodges, C., Moore, S., Lockee, B., Trust, T., & Bond, A. (2020, March 27). The difference between emergency remote teaching and online learning. *Educause Review, 27*(1), 1–9.

Holmes, A., & Zubak, C. (2015, April 1). *U.S. internet users pay more and have fewer choices than Europeans.* The Center for Public Integrity. https://www.publicintegrity.org/2015/04/01/16998/us-internet-users-pay-more-and-have-fewerchoices-europeans

Hsieh, Y. H., & Tsai, C. C. (2012). The effect of moderator's facilitative strategies on online synchronous discussions. *Computers in Human Behavior*, *28*(5), 1708–1716. http://dx.doi.org/10.1016/j.chb.2012.04.010

Hurtado, S., Alvarado, A. R., & Guillermo-Wann, C. (2015). Thinking about race: The salience of racial identity at two- and four-year colleges and the climate for diversity. *The Journal of Higher Education*, *86*(1), 127–155.

Hypolite, L. I. (2020). People, place, and connections: Black cultural center staff as facilitators of social capital. *Journal of Black Studies*, *51*(1), 37–59. https://doi.org/10.1177/0021934719892238

Jacobi, L. (2017). The structure of discussions in an online communication Course: What do students find most effective? *Journal of University Teaching & Learning Practice*, *14*(1), 11. https://ro.uow.edu.au/jutlp/vol14/iss1/11/

Johnson, H. (2016, June 28). *The rise and fall of enrollment at for-profit colleges*. Public Policy Institute of California. www.ppic.org/blog/the-rise-and-fall-of-enrollment-at-for-profit-colleges/

Joyner, D. A., Wang, Q., Thakare, S., Jing, S., Goel, A., & MacIntyre, B. (2020, August). The synchronicity paradox in online education. In *Proceedings of the Seventh ACM Conference on Learning@ Scale*. ACM Digital Library. https://doi.org/10.1145/3386527.3405922

Ke, F., & Hoadley, C. (2009). Evaluating online learning communities. *Educational Technology Research and Development*, *57*(4), 487–510. https://doi.org/10.1007/s11423-009-9120-2

Kendi, I. X. (2019). *How to be an antiracist*. One World.

Koehler, M., & Mishra, P. (2009). What is technological pedagogical content knowledge (TPACK)? *Contemporary issues in technology and teacher education*, *9*(1), 60–70.

Knapp, N. F. (2018). Increasing interaction in a flipped online classroom through video conferencing. *TechTrends*, *62*(6), 618–624. https://doi.org/10.1007/s11528-018-0336-z

Lai, K. W. (2015). Knowledge construction in online learning communities: A case study of a doctoral course. *Studies in Higher Education*, *40*(4), 561–579. https://doi.org/10.1080/03075079.2013.831402

Larmer, J., & Mergendoller, J. R. (2010). Seven essentials for project-based learning. *Educational leadership*, *68*(1), 34–37.

Lee, J. S., Blackwell, S., Drake, J., & Moran, K. A. (2014). Taking a leap of faith: Redefining teaching and learning in higher education through project-based learning. *Interdisciplinary Journal of Problem-Based Learning*, *8*(2), 2. https://doi.org/10.7771/1541-5015.1426

Lin, X., & Gao, L. (2020). Students' sense of community and perspectives of taking synchronous and asynchronous online courses. *Asian Journal of Distance Education*, *15*(1), 169–179. http://www.asianjde. org/ojs/index.php/AsianJDE/article/view/448

Lowenthal, P., Borup, J., West, R., & Archambault, L. (2020). Thinking beyond Zoom: Using asynchronous video to maintain connection and engagement during the COVID-19 pandemic. *Journal of Technology and Teacher Education, 28*(2), 383–391. https://www.learntechlib.org/primary/p/216192/

Martin, F., & Bolliger, D. (2018). Engagement matters: Student perceptions on the importance of engagement strategies in the online learning environment. *Online Learning, 22*(1), 205–222. https://doi.org/10.24059/olj.v22i1.1092

Martin, F., & Parker, M. A. (2014). Use of synchronous virtual classrooms: Why, who, and how. *MERLOT Journal of Online Learning and Teaching, 10*(2), 192–210.

McDaniels, M., Pfund, C., & Barnicle, K. (2016). Creating dynamic learning communities in synchronous online courses: One approach from the center for the integration of research, teaching, and learning (CIRTL). *Online Learning, 20*(1), 110–129. http://dx.doi.org/10.24059/olj.v20i1.518

McMillan, D. W., & Chavis, D. M. (1986). Sense of community: A definition and theory. *Journal of community psychology, 14*(1), 6–23. https://doi.org/10.1002/1520-6629(198601)14:1<6::AID-JCOP2290140103>3.0.CO;2-I

Milman, N. B. (2020, March 25). Pandemic pedagogy. *Phi Delta Kappan, 25.* https://kappanonline.org/pandemic-pedagogy-covid-19-online-milman/

Mitchell, D. D. (2006). Flashcard: Alternating between visible and invisible identities. *Equity & Excellence in Education, 39*(2), 137–145. https://www.tandfonline.com/doi/abs/10.1080/10665680600580132

Müller, T. (2008). Persistence of women in online degree-completion programs. *International Review of Research in Open and Distributed Learning, 9*(2), 1–18.

National Center on Accessible Educational Materials. (2021, May 10). *Pour accessibility on your oer curation & authoring*. AEM Center. https://aem.cast.org/get-started/events/2019/11/pour-accessibility-oer-curation

Olesova, L., Slavin, M., & Lim, J. (2016). Exploring the effect of scripted roles on cognitive presence in asynchronous online discussions. *Online Learning, 20*(4), 34–53. https://olj.onlinelearningconsortium.org/

Ozan, O., & Ozarslan, Y. (2016). Video lecture watching behaviors of learners in online courses. *Educational Media International, 53*(1), 27–41. https://doi.org/10.1080/09523987.2016.1189255

Patton, L. D., & Harper, S. R. (2003). Mentoring relationships among African American women in graduate and professional schools. In M. F. Howard-Hamilton (Ed.), *Meeting the Needs of African American Women* (New Directions for Student Services, no. 104, pp. 67–78). Jossey Bass. https://doi.org/10.1002/ss.108

Peña, E. V., Stapleton, L. D., & Schaffer, L. M. (2016). Critical perspectives on disability identity. In E. S. Abes (Ed.), *Critical and Diverse Perspectives on College Student Development Theory* (New Directions for Student Services, no. 154, pp. 85–96). Jossey-Bass.

Pena-Shaff, J., & Altman, W. (2015). Student interaction and knowledge construction in case-based learning in educational psychology using online discussions: The role of structure. *Journal of Interactive Learning Research, 26*(3), 307–329.

Petty, T., & Farinde, A. (2013). Investigating student engagement in an online mathematics course through windows into teaching and learning. *Journal of Online Learning and Teaching, 9*(2), 261–270. https://jolt.merlot.org/vol9no2/petty_0613.pdf

Price, D. V., & Tovar, E. (2014). Student engagement and institutional graduation rates: Identifying high-impact educational practices for community colleges. *Community College Journal of Research and Practice, 38*(9), 766–782. https://doi.org/10.1080/10668926.2012.719481

Pyhältö, K., Stubb, J., & Lonka, K. (2009). Developing scholarly communities as learning environments for doctoral students. *International Journal for Academic Development, 14*(3), 221–232.

Redden, E. (2020, March 26). Zoombombers' disrupt online classes with racist, pornographic content. *Inside Higher Ed.* https://www.insidehighered.com/news/2020/03/26/zoombombers-disrupt-online-classes-racist-pornographic-content.

Ribera, A. K., Miller, A. L., & Dumford, A. D. (2017). Sense of peer belonging and institutional acceptance in the first year: The role of high-impact practices. *Journal of College Student Development, 58*(4), 545–563. https://doi.org/10.1353/csd.2017.0042

Riggs, S. A., & Linder, K. E. (2016). Actively engaging students in asynchronous online classes. *Idea, 64*, 1–10. https://www.ideaedu.org/Portals/0/Uploads/Documents/IDEA%20Papers/IDEA%20Papers/PaperIDEA_64.pdf

Rosenberg, M., & McCullough, B. C. (1981). Mattering: Inferred significance and mental health among adolescents. *Research in Community & Mental Health, 2*, 163–182.

Rovai, A. (2003). In search of higher persistence rates in distance education online programs. *The Internet and Higher Education, 6*(1), 1–16. http://dx.doi.org/10.1016/S1096-7516(02)00158-6

Rudd, D. P. II, & Rudd, D. P. (2014). The value of video in online instruction. *Journal of Instructional Pedagogies, 13*, 1–7. https://files.eric.ed.gov/fulltext/EJ1060143.pdf

Ryan, C. (2018, August). Computer and internet use in the United States: 2016. *American Community Survey Reports*, ACS-39, U.S. Census Bureau, Washington, DC. https://www.census.gov/content/dam/Census/library/publications/2018/acs/ACS-39.pdf

Saltz, J., & Heckman, R. (2020). Using structured pair activities in a distributed online breakout room. *Online Learning, 24*(1), 227–244. https://files.eric.ed.gov/fulltext/EJ1249342.pdf

Stanford, D. (2020, March 16). *Videoconferencing alternative: How low-bandwidth teaching will save us all.* iddblog. https://www.iddblog.org/videoconferencing-alternatives-how-low-bandwidth-teaching-will-save-us-all/

Strayhorn, T. L. (2012). *College students' sense of belonging: A key to educational success for all students.* Routledge.

Stringer, E. T. (2008). *Action research in education*. Pearson Prentice Hall.
Stubb, J., Pyhältö, K., & Lonka, K. (2011). Balancing between inspiration and exhaustion: PhD students' experienced socio-psychological well-being. *Studies in Continuing Education, 33*(1), 33–50.
Tinto, V. (1997). Classrooms as communities: Exploring the educational character of student persistence. *The Journal of Higher Education, 68*(6), 599–623.
Torres-Harding, S., Diaz, E., Schaumberger, A., & Carrollo, O. (2015). Psychological sense of community and university mission as predictors of student social justice engagement. *Journal of Higher Education Outreach and Engagement, 19*(3), 89–112. https://www.researchgate.net/publication/290446155_Psychological_Sense_of_Community_and_University_Mission_as_Predictors_of_Student_Social_Justice_Engagement
Turner, S. D. (2016). *Digital denied: The impact of systemic racial discrimination on home-internet adoption*. FreePress. https://www.freepress.net/sites/default/files/legacy-policy/digital_denied_free_press_report_december_2016.pdf
Ukpokodu, O. N. (2008). Teachers' reflections on pedagogies that enhance learning in an online course on teaching for equity and social justice. *Journal of Interactive Online Learning, 7*(3), 227–255.
U.S. Department of Education. (2008). *Higher Education Opportunity Act 2008*. Law & Guidance / Higher Education. https://www2.ed.gov/policy/highered/leg/hea08/index.html
U.S. Department of Education, National Center for Education Statistics. (2021). *Digest of education statistics, 2019* (2021-009). Table 311.10. https://nces.ed.gov/pubs2021/2021009.pdf
U.S. Government Accountability Office. (2016, April 27). *Tribal internet access: Increased federal coordination and performance measurement needed*. https://www.gao.gov/products/gao-16-504t
vanOostveen, R., Childs, E., Gerbrandt, J., & Awwadah, K. (2018, October 16–18). *Explorations of social immediacy/intimacy in fully online learning communities while using synchronous tools* [Paper presentation]. Online Learning Global Summit and EdTech Expo, Teaching and Learning in the Digital Age; Toronto, ON, Canada. https://www.researchgate.net/publication/349380468_Exploring_social_immediacyintimacy_in_fully_online_learning_communities_through_synchronous_tools
Veletsianos, G., Houlden, S., Hodson, J., & Gosse, C. (2018, June 22). Women scholars' experiences with online harassment and abuse: Self-protection, resistance, acceptance, and self-blame. *New Media & Society, 20*(12), 4689–4708. https://doi.org/10.1177/1461444818781324
Veletsianos, G., & Kimmons, R. (2016). Scholars in an increasingly digital and open world: How do education professors and students use Twitter? *The Internet and Higher Education, 30*(2016), 1–10. https://www.veletsianos.com/wp-content/uploads/2011/07/scholars_open_twitter_inPress.pdf

Vogels, E. A. (2021, October 19). *Some digital divides persist between rural, urban and Suburban America*. Pew Research Center. https://www.pewresearch.org/fact-tank/2021/08/19/some-digital-divides-persist-between-rural-urban-and-suburban-america/

Walker, C. (2015). An analysis of cyberbullying among sexual minority university students. *Journal of Higher Education Theory and Practice, 15*(7), 44. http://m.www.na-businesspress.com/JHETP/WalkerC_Web15_7_.pdf

Wheaton College Massachusetts. (2020, August 28). *The gender-affirming classroom*. https://wheatoncollege.edu/campus-life/social-justice-community-impact/lgbtq/the-network/creating-a-gender-affirming-wheaton-a-guide/the-gender-affirming-classroom/.

World Health Organization. (2019, May 28). *Burn-out an "Occupational phenomenon": International Classification of Diseases.* https://www.who.int/news/item/28-05-2019-burn-out-an-occupational-phenomenon-international-classification-of-diseases

Yamagata-Lynch, L. C. (2014). Blending online asynchronous and synchronous learning. *International Review of Research in Open and Distributed Learning, 15*(2), 189–212.

Yuan, J., & Kim, C. (2014). Guidelines for facilitating the development of learning communities in online courses. *Journal of Computer Assisted Learning, 30*(3), 220–232. https://onlinelibrary.wiley.com/doi/10.1111/jcal.12042

Zhu, X., Chen, B., Avadhanam, R. M., Shui, H., & Zhang, R. Z. (2020). Reading and connecting: Using social annotation in online classes. *Information and Learning Sciences, 121*(5/6), 261–271. https://doi.org/10.1108/ILS-04-2020-0117

Zyngier, D. (2008). (Re)conceptualising student engagement: Doing education not doing time. *Teaching and Teacher Education, 24*(7), 1765–1776. https://doi.org/10.1016/j.tate.2007.09.004

ABOUT THE AUTHOR

Sharla E. Berry, PhD is a faculty member in the field of education leadership and an expert in the field of digital equity and online learning. Her research has been featured in many academic journals including *Online Learning* and the *International Review of Research in Open and Distributed Learning*, and at academic conferences including the American Educational Research Association (AERA) and the Association for the Study of Higher Education (ASHE). Sharla is committed to using her research to support practitioners in teaching and leading with technology. Various groups have invited her to do keynote speeches and workshops, including the Los Angeles Unified School District's Instructional Technology Initiative and the Los Angeles Community College District. In 2022, she was recognized as one of the International Society for Technology in Education (ISTE)'s "20 to Watch." With each unique speech or workshop, Sharla helps practitioners imagine a digitally equitable future, one that helps students of diverse racial, ethnic, and socioeconomic backgrounds achieve their highest aspirations.

INDEX

ableism, 17
achievement data, within LMS, 45
Action Research, 34
administrators
    asynchronous course considerations for, 80–82
    community considerations for, 20
    crisis role of, 105–106
    faculty collaboration with, 81–82
    online instruction considerations for, 35–36
    synchronous course considerations for, 96
    technology considerations for, 59–61
Adobe Connect, 49
affordances concept, 60
African American students, 12, 17
American Indian Alaska Native students, 17, 57
antiracism, 32–33
Asian students, 17
asynchronous courses
    asynchronous video within, 46–47, 49
    blogs within, 65, 67
    collaboration within, 66–67
    community within, 42, 44, 46–49, 66–67
    considerations for, 40
    digital social reading and annotation within, 64–65, 67
    discussion boards within, 39, 46, 67–74
    for emergency remote teaching (ERT), 105
    flexibility within, 39–40, 44
    graphic organizers within, 64
    instructor-led, 39
    learning activities within, 64–66
    learning opportunities within, 43, 46–49
    orientation of, 63
    overview of, 39, 63–64
    podcasts within, 66, 67
    portfolios within, 66, 67
    quizzes and tests within, 65
    reflection within, 66
    scaffolding within, 64
    self-guided, 39
    strengths of, 39–40
    student-instructor interactions within, 64–66
    supplemental support within, 81
    in time of crisis, 44
    tools for, 48–49
    video feedback within, 47–48, 49
    wikis within, 65, 67
asynchronous video, 46–47, 49

bandwidth, 57, 58
belonging, 1–2, 3, 12–13
bias, 80
Black, Indigenous, and People of Color (BIPOC) students
    within asynchronous environments, 80
    belonging and, 12–13
    community creation strategies for, 19
    disability and, 18
    hashtags for, 14
    inclusion for, 32–33
    in-person meeting benefits to, 8

mental health disorders within, 103
in online courses and programs, 12–14
racialized experiences of, 13
term use of, 9
Blackboard collaborate, 49
Black Cultural Centers, 13
Black women scholars, harassment to, 16
blended courses (hybrid courses), 38–39, 41–42, 43, 44
blogs, 65, 67
breakout rooms, 54, 55, 92–95
broadband, access challenges to, 12
burnout, 106

case study learning activity, 91–92
Center for Applied Special Technology (CAST), 31
chat rooms, 25, 51–53, 55, 87
clarifications, as peer facilitation, 78
cocurriculum, significance of, 8
cognitive fatigue, 51
collaboration, 26–28, 66–67, 89, 92–95
collaborative assessment, 89
collaborative writing, 89
comments, within discussion boards, 76–77
community
  academic benefits of, 3–4
  within asynchronous courses, 42, 44, 46–49, 66–67
  belonging within, 1–2
  challenges to, 4–5
  within COVID-19 pandemic, 103–107
  creating, 2–3
  defined, 1
  within discussion boards, 68–69
  emotional benefits of, 4
  experience within, 2
  feelings of, 1
  as frame, 99–100
  fulfillment within, 1
  influence within, 1
  learning, 4
  membership within, 1
  online, 5–8, 14–16
  within online courses, 42–44
  peer facilitation and, 78–79
  shared emotional connection within, 1
  social benefits of, 3–4
  strategies for, 18–19
  within synchronous courses, 41, 42, 54, 85–86
  through social media, 7
  of underrepresented students, 4
  within video conferencing, 50–51, 54
  work within, 2
community of inquiry (COI) framework, 5–6, 35
conduct, on discussion boards, 73
connection promotion, as peer facilitation, 78
correspondence courses, 39
COVID-19 pandemic, 44, 100–101, 103–107
cultural centers, 13–14
cyberbullying, 15

deadnaming, 29
digital social reading and annotation, 64–65, 67
disabilities, students with, 17–18, 19, 31, 54–56
#disabilitysowhite, 18
discussion boards
  within asynchronous courses, 39, 46, 67–74
  benefits of, 68
  challenges regarding, 70
  comment use within, 76–77
  community agreements regarding, 73
  community within, 68–69
  conduct regarding, 73

expectations regarding, 71
gender bias within, 80
generative prompts on, 73–74
grading process regarding, 70, 72
instructor moderators on, 74–75
learning opportunities within, 49
management of, 74–77
moderating of, 74–75
organization within, 75
peer facilitation within, 77–79
peer-to-peer response within, 71–72
race bias within, 80
role play within, 79–80
routines regarding, 75
rubrics for, 72
structure of, 76
student participation within, 70, 75, 76
within synchronous courses, 89
teaching strategies regarding, 79–80
technology choices regarding, 70
types of, 68, 69
use of, 25–26, 68
video threads within, 76
diversity, 9
diversity, equity, and inclusion (DEI), 33–34, 56–58. *See also* inclusion

Edconnect, 47
educational communities, creating, 2–3
email, 23, 25–26
emergency remote teaching (ERT), 104–105
engagement
  in breakout rooms, 93
  defined, 3
  in discussion boards, 70, 75, 76
  by students, 3, 50, 90
  within synchronous courses, 41, 90
  within virtual classroom, 50
equity, in technology, 56–58
equity audit, of syllabi, 30
equity-minded approach, 10–11

faculty
  administrator collaboration with, 81–82
  breakout room role of, 93
  burnout of, 106
  characteristics of, 34–35
  community considerations for, 20
  crisis role of, 105
  cyberbullying and, 15–16
  DEI learning activities of, 33
  digital social reading and annotation of, 64–65
  as discussion board moderators, 74–75, 89
  within educational communities, 2
  equity-minded approaches of, 10–11
  online instruction considerations for, 36–37
  role play by, 79–80
  synchronous course considerations for, 97
  technology considerations for, 61–62, 82
  video feedback from, 47–48
family, challenges regarding, 14
female students, 14–15, 19, 103. *See also* women
fishbowl activity, 91
flexibility, 39–40, 44, 104–105
Flipgrid, 47, 63
flipped classroom model, 87
Floyd, George, 32
fulfillment, 1

gender, 14–16
gender affirming classes, 31–32
gender bias, 80
gender inclusive language, 29
generative prompts, on discussion boards, 73–74
grading, discussion boards and, 70, 72
graphic organizers, 64

harassment, 16, 59

hashtags, for BIPOC, 14
hearing impaired students, 95–96
high impact practices, 13
Hispanic students, 17
hybrid courses (blended courses), 38–39, 41–42, 43, 44

ice-breaker discussion board, 69
icebreakers, 85
idea exchange, 26
identity-based peer networks, 13
immediacy, 58
inclusion, 10–11, 30–34
influence, 1
information provision, 79, 104
in-person connections, 8
instructional designers
    asynchronous course considerations for, 82
    community considerations for, 20
    online instruction considerations for, 36–37
    synchronous course considerations for, 97
    technology considerations for, 61–62
instructor-led asynchronous course, 39
integrated framework for community, 7–8
internet speed, 57
intersectionality, 9
introduction discussion board, 69
introductions, student, 23–24
introductory video, 23

language, gender inclusive, 29
Latinx students, 12
learning community, 4. *See also* community
learning management system (LMS), 39, 45–46, 63, 70
learning opportunities
    of asynchronous courses, 43, 46–49
    of asynchronous video, 49
    of breakout rooms, 55

    of chat feature, 51–53, 55
    of discussion boards, 49
    of hybrid courses, 43
    of polls, 55
    of synchronous courses, 43
    of video conferencing, 50–51, 55
    of video feedback, 49
    of virtual whiteboards, 55
lecture, within synchronous courses, 87–88
LGBTQ students, 15, 16, 31–32, 103
low-income students, 11 12, 19, 56–58, 103

marginalization, 4
marginalized students, 18–19, 28–29, 95–96. *See also specific types*
membership, 1
mental health, 103, 105–106
microaggressions, 4
minorities, defined, 9
mobile devices, information access on, 104
mode of instruction, choosing, 44

National Center on Accessible Educational Materials (AEM), 55
nonbinary students, 31–32

online community, 5–8, 14–16. *See also* community
online courses/programs
    antiracism and, 32–33
    BIPOC students within, 12–14
    chat feature within, 51–53
    collaboration within, 26
    community formation through, 5
    community within, 42–44
    diversity in, 11–12
    harassment within, 59
    high impact practices within, 13
    hybrid courses (blended courses), 38–39, 41–42, 43, 44
    icebreakers within, 85

idea exchange within, 26
inclusive framework need within, 8–11
mode of instruction choice within, 44
peer interactions within, 85
personal and professional updates within, 24–25
social presence within, 22–26
soft starts within, 24, 84–85
student communication within, 25–26
students with disabilities in, 17–18
syllabi for, 30
temporality within, 38–39, 42–44
usage data from, 45
virtual classroom functions within, 25
water cooler sessions within, 24, 85
See also asynchronous courses; synchronous courses
orientation, of asynchronous courses, 63
the outsider within, 4

Pacific Islander students, 17
pandemic pedagogy, 106–107
parking lots discussion board, 69
pedagogical knowledge, 21
peer facilitation, 28, 77–79
peer interaction discussion board, 69
peer-to-peer interaction, 6, 24, 71–72
perceivable, operable, understandable and robust (POUR) framework, 31, 54–56
podcasts, 66, 67
polls, 53, 54, 55, 89
portfolios, 66, 67
post-assessment discussion board, 69
pre-assessment discussion board, 69
precollege experiences, 6
presences, 5
problem-based learning activity, 92
program evaluation, as collaborative activity, 28

project-based learning (PBL), 33–34, 92

question and answer forums discussion board, 69
questioning, as peer facilitation, 78
quizzes, 65

race bias, 80
reflection, 66
remote students, 56–58
role play, within discussion boards, 79–80
rubrics, 72
rural students, 11–12, 56–58

Saba Centra, 49
safety, 28–29, 61
scaffolding, within asynchronous courses, 64
self-guided asynchronous course, 39
sexual minority students, 15–16, 19
shared emotional connection, 1
shared resource creation, 28
social class, 9–10
social cues, as peer facilitation, 79
socialization discussion board, 69
social media, 7, 15
social presence, 22–26, 84
Socratic questioning, 79–80
soft starts, 24, 84–85
staff
    asynchronous course considerations for, 82
    community considerations for, 20
    cyberbullying role of, 15–16
    within educational communities, 2–3
    online instruction considerations for, 36–37
    synchronous course considerations for, 97
    technology considerations for, 61–62
structured pair activity (SPA) model, 94

student-instructor interactions, within asynchronous courses, 64–66
students
 burnout of, 106
 communication with, 25–26
 community benefits to, 3–4
 community creation strategies for, 18–19
 discussion board engagement by, 70, 75, 76
 within educational communities, 2
 engagement by, 3, 50, 90
 introduction space for, 23–24
 offline connections by, 7–8
 online program experiences of, 6
 personal and professional updates by, 24–25
 precollege experiences of, 6
 presences to, 5
 safety for, 28–29
 support services for, 8
 underrepresented, 4
 See also Black, Indigenous, and People of Color (BIPOC) students; *specific types*
students with disabilities, 17–18, 19, 31
summarizing, as peer facilitation, 79
support services, 8
syllabi, equity audit of, 30
synchronous courses
 administrator considerations within, 96
 agenda use within, 85–86
 asynchronous learning activities within, 88–89
 breakout rooms within, 92–95
 case study activity within, 91–92
 chat use within, 87
 collaborative assessment within, 89
 collaborative learning activities within, 90–92
 collaborative writing within, 89
 community within, 41, 42, 54, 85–86
 considerations for, 41
 discussion boards within, 89
 discussion within, 87–88
 for emergency remote teaching (ERT), 105
 engagement within, 41
 fishbowl activity within, 91
 flipped classroom model within, 87
 hearing impaired students within, 95–96
 learning opportunities within, 43
 lecture time within, 87–88
 marginalized student considerations within, 95–96
 organization of, 85–86
 overview of, 38, 40, 84–85
 peer interaction within, 88
 polls within, 53, 89
 problem-based/project-based learning within, 92
 soft starts within, 84–85
 strengths of, 41
 structure of, 40, 85–86
 student role within, 90
 technology use within, 86–87
 think-pair-share activity within, 91
 in time of crisis, 44
 tools for, 49–50
 underrepresented student considerations within, 95–96
 video conferencing use within, 86–87
 visually impaired students within, 95–96

task mastery, 27
teaching, influences to, 21
technical knowledge, 21
technology
 considerations regarding, 59–62
 equity considerations regarding, 56–58
 expectations and norms regarding, 86–87

immediacy of, 58
integration of, 21
POUR framework and, 54–56
for virtual classrooms, 50
See also specific types
technology access, 12
temporality, within online courses, 38–39, 42–44
tests, within asynchronous courses, 65
theory of persistence, in distance education programs, 6
think-pair-share learning activity, 91
tribal students, 11–12

underrepresented students, 4, 18–19, 28–29, 95–96. *See also specific types*
universal design for learning (UDL), 31
usage data, within LMS, 45

video, asynchronous, 46–47, 49
video conferencing, 50–51, 54, 55, 86–87. *See also* online courses/programs

video feedback, 47–48, 49
virtual classroom, 25, 49–50, 51–53. *See also* online courses/programs
virtual whiteboards, 54, 55
visually impaired students, 95–96

water cooler discussions, 24, 85
Web Accessibility Initiative (WAI), 55
Web conferencing software, 49
WebEx, 49
welcome letter, 23
Wheaton College, 32
wikis, 65, 67
women, 14–16, 31–32. *See also* female students
writing, collaborative, 89
writing activities, 33

Zoom, 49
Zoom bombings, 59
Zoom fatigue, 51

For Product Safety Concerns and Information please contact our EU representative GPSR@taylorandfrancis.com
Taylor & Francis Verlag GmbH, Kaufingerstraße 24, 80331 München, Germany

www.ingramcontent.com/pod-product-compliance
Lightning Source LLC
Chambersburg PA
CBHW052025290426
44112CB00014B/2387